Bill — to Tessa

Dear Russell's,
Hope you visit Israel!
with all my love. OVA

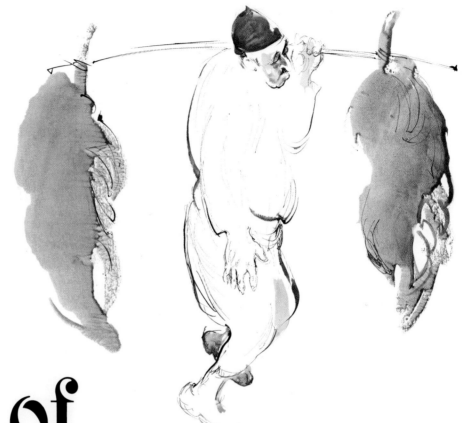

People of
Old Jerusalem

by Papas.

Holt, Rinehart and Winston   New York

The Old City of Jerusalem

Copyright © 1980 by William Papas

Published by Holt, Rinehart and Winston,
383 Madison Avenue, New York, N.Y. 10017.

Library of Congress Cataloging in Publication Data

ISBN 0 03 057483 8
LC 80 197
First Edition
Designer: Marian Morris
Printed in Great Britain
10 9 8 7 6 5 4 3 2 1

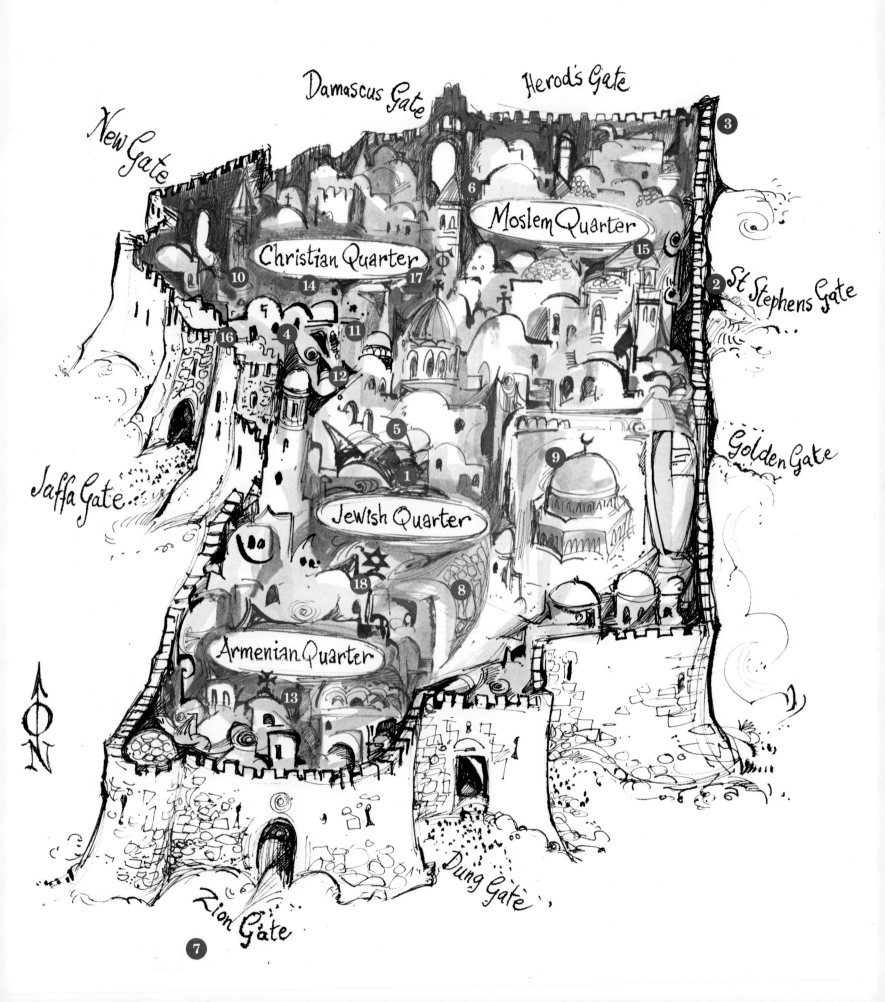

Damascus Gate

Herod's Gate

New Gate

⑥

Moslem Quarter

Christian Quarter

⑮

⑩   ⑭   ⑰

② St Stephens Gate

⑯   ④   ⑪

⑫

⑤

⑨

Golden Gate

①

Jewish Quarter

Jaffa Gate

⑱   ⑧

Armenian Quarter

⑬

③

Dung Gate

Zion Gate

⑦

N

Preface

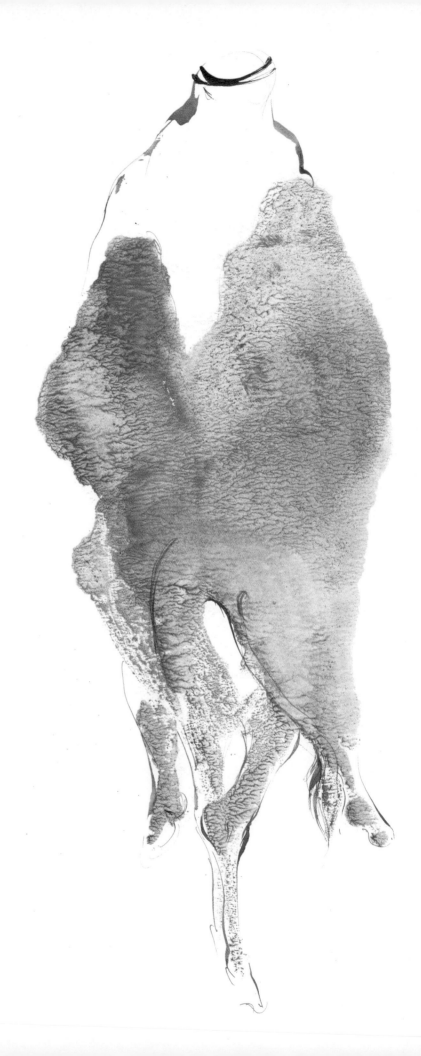

My home during my stay in Jerusalem was Mishkenot Sha' ananim, once the first Jewish suburb outside the Old City walls, now a guest house sponsored by the Jerusalem Foundation to which artists, writers and musicians from everywhere are invited to stay in order to work or relax. I thank the Foundation for their generosity in loaning my wife, Tessa, and me an apartment and studio, and the helpful and friendly custodians of Mishkenot who made our stay so pleasant.

We spent three months in these convenient surroundings, only a hundred metres or so from the Jaffa Gate. Every morning I would walk through the gardens, past the porters, under the arches of the Jaffa Gate and into the Old City. I thought I was getting to know it well but each day would open another undiscovered door leading to a new experience that would trigger off yet another opening to other people.

During my first excursions the inhabitants were suspicious. They could not categorize me as I was obviously not a tourist. But as the drawings progressed I became established. 'Hey, why

Temple Market

don't you draw me?', 'Where are you going? Sit down and have coffee.' And in a strange way I too became part of the city, a character in my own right.

But by the time I was to leave it struck me how shallow my excavations really were. On the other hand, I was left with many vivid, startling impressions. It is these I have tried to record in this book.

Papas.

Abraham started it. From the time he offered Isaac as a sacrifice on the sacred Rock people have struggled to reach Jerusalem, a city without water, surrounded by mountains, strategically unimportant and commercially unsound. David was among the first. He bought land from the Jebusites and built his city to the south east of the present walls. Solomon followed and built a great temple. It housed the Ark, holiest symbol of the Israelites and the focus of Judaism.

Pilgrims came and inevitably invaders; Sennacherib and his Assyrians, Nebuchadnezzar of the Babylonians, names that evoke bloodshed and devastation and the first diaspora for the people of Israel. But however far they scattered there was always Jerusalem, the symbol of their faith.

After the arrival of a tolerant ruler, Cyrus the Great of Persia, the Israelites returned and rebuilt their Temple.

Other agressors came.

Alexander the Great and his Greeks, Egyptian Ptolemies, and the Seleucids of Syria with their Hellenistic ideals and quarrels; Jewish High Priests and Kings, Oniads and Tobiads, Pharisees and Sadducees, Hasmonaeans, descendants of the heroic Maccabees. There was the time of Essenes disillusioned with the Hellenization of Judaism, of conspiracies and slaughter and torture until Herod the Great, appointed by the Roman general Pompey, brought a period of peace and prosperity to Jerusalem.

Herod died and a series of Roman procurators ruled the city. During Roman rule a Jew from Nazareth entered the city. According to the Gospels he was condemned by the High Priests, judged by Pontius Pilate, the fifth Procurator, crucified on the hill of Golgotha and ascended to Heaven a few weeks later. Jerusalem had a new symbol, the Cross, and a new faith, Christianity. Pilate was banished and Herod's grandson, Herod Agrippa I took his place. On his death Jerusalem returned to turmoil. The Zealots threw the Romans out twice, but fought each other, Jew against Jew, until the exasperated Romans razed the city to the ground. Aelia Capitolina grew from the ashes, the Temple was destroyed and the Jews banned and dispersed.

Christianity spread, became a recognized religion, and the Byzantines, Greeks and Armenians arrived, led by Emperor Constantine and his

mother, Helena. Aelia Capitolina gave up its pagan shrines and become Jerusalem once more, city of Christ's crucifixion and resurrection. Helena, guided so she claimed by divine vision, located all the Christian sites within the city. Under her direction the Church of the Holy Sepulchre rose over the tomb of Christ. The Jews were still banned but pilgrims from the West and East flocked to this new bastion of Christian faith. But more aggressors were on their way. The Sassanians of Persia, aided by the Jews and Samaritans, conquered Jerusalem and once more the city was reduced to ruins. Heraclius negotiated a truce, the Byzantines return-ed and the city wearily awaited the next invasion.

In the deserts to the south the third great religion was gathering momentum. The followers of Mohammed and Islam launched a *Jihad*, a holy war, and brilliantly outmanoeuvring the Byzantine armies, overran the Middle East, from Persia in the east to the Mediterranean in the west.

Caliph Omar arrived in Jerusalem. He was met by the Greek Orthodox Patriarch, Sophronius, who escorted him to the site of Solomon's Temple. Omar decreed that a mosque be built to house the Rock, sacred to the Moslems because from it Mohammed had ascended to the seventh Heaven. Jerusalem became the city of three faiths, three creeds, three animosities.

The Ommayyads proved wise and tolerant rulers. There was little bloodshed, the Jews were allowed to return to the city, and both they and the Christians could pray in their synagogues and churches. The Ommayyads reasoned that all Moslems, Christians and Jews were People of the Book and could live together in peace and harmony. This was not to be. The Crusaders started to smash their bloody way down the Rhine,

Israeli Soldier in Riot Gear.

massacring thousands of Jews: their destination Jerusalem, their objective to rid the holy Christian places of infidels and the murderers of Christ.

Two years later they arrived at the gates of Jerusalem, and by nightfall all Moslems and most Jews, young and old, had been slaughtered. The streets were piled high with corpses; a sorry contrast with the previous take-over of the city. The Crusaders declared Jerusalem capital of Palestine, themselves kings. Christian pilgrims thronged to the city but only one Jew came. Judah Halevi reached the gates from Cairo but was ridden down by a horseman before he could enter.

One hundred years later the Frankish kingdom was in disarray; torn by revolts and rifts it was easy for Saladin and his Moslem armies to restore Palestine and Jerusalem to Moslem rule. As brutal as the Crusaders had been, so merciful was Saladin. He spared all Christian lives save the Templars who had desecrated the sacred Temple Mount. Jerusalem was once more in the hands of Islam and would remain that way for the next eight hundred years. The

CHWEIPI.
ELECTRONICS.

3900 in the
chweipi family.
Some Muslims
& Some Jewish

רחוב שוק הלחמים

شارع السوق اللحامين

SUQ. EL-LAHHAMIN

Maria from Athens
(Greek Nun)

cloth
seller.

orthodox Christians were delighted to see the last of the fanatical Latins and the Church of the Holy Sepulchre was restored to them. The Jews too, persecuted in most European countries, started to return and from that time on there has been a steady stream heading for their holy city.

Then came the Tartars, brief occupiers until the city fell to the Mameluk sultans of Egypt.

Bedonne Laly

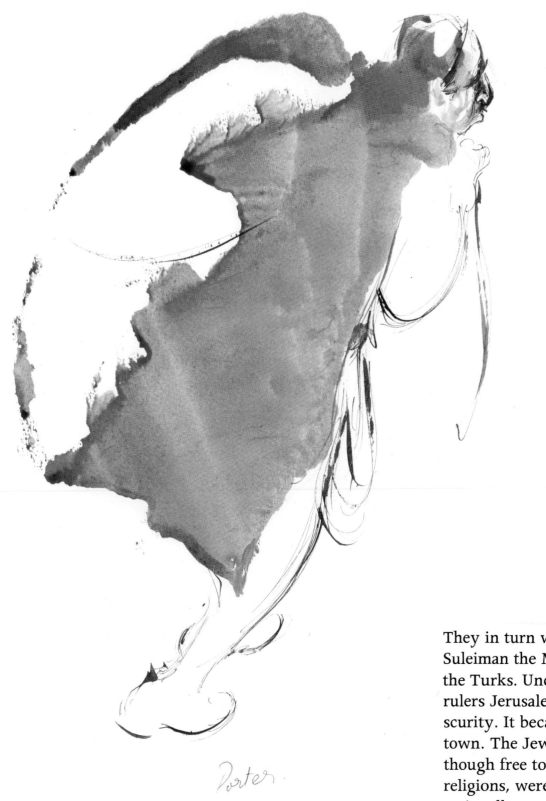

Porter.

They in turn were defeated by Suleiman the Magnificent and the Turks. Under these new rulers Jerusalem sank into obscurity. It became a poor, dirty town. The Jews and Christians, though free to practise their religions, were harassed, occasionally murdered and made to pay exorbitant taxes. A tannery was built next to the Church of the Holy Sepulchre, a

slaughterhouse next to the Ben Zakkai synagogue 'so that an evil smell should ever plague the infidel'.

But such was the meaning of Jerusalem for both Jews and Christians that people continued to make the arduous journey and many settled there. By the turn of the twentieth century the population had grown to about 50,000 of whom the majority were Jewish. Towards the end of the First World War the Turks were driven from Jerusalem by General Allenby and the victorious British army.

The British became the new rulers of Palestine and Jerusalem was made its capital. Zionism was born in the diaspora with Theodor Herzl's book *The Jewish State* (1896) the catalyst. Encouraged by the Balfour Declaration, which stated the British Government's intention to help establish a national home for the Jewish people, Jews flocked to their ancient land and to Jerusalem. Tensions grew as more Jews poured into the country and Arab discontent exploded in riots, fueled by Moslem religious leaders who told their followers that the Jews had designs on the Moslem holy

EL WAD
Turning into the Via Dolorosa.

places. The British imposed a quota on the number of Jewish immigrants but by 1940 groups of Arabs and Jewish terrorists were killing each other as well as the British. These squirmishes led to the eventual exodus of the British, the creation of the State of Israel, open warfare between Arab and Jew and the partition of Jerusalem.

The Jordanians took the Old City, all Jews were expelled and half the Jewish Quarter was destroyed. Neither Israeli Jews nor Israeli Arabs were permitted to visit their holy places for twenty years.

1967 and the Six Day War; once more the streets of Jerusalem were a battlefield, Arab against Jew, but this time it was the Israelis who triumphantly entered the Old City. Jerusalem was a whole city again. Jews, Arabs and Christians were completely free to practise their religion at their holy places. Jerusalem was once more a city of three faiths.

Spring Onion
Seller.—

The old city is a kaleido-
scope. Of faces, from
black African to pale
Nordic, of costumes,
jellabas, gowns, cassocks,
uniforms; of colours, golds, silver,
deep reds, blues and blacks,
earth tones of vegetable and
fruit, rawness of bloody meat,
glistening white and honey
stickiness of sweets, all against
a backdrop of dun stone. A
shake and the pattern changes
to sound and smell; freshly
baked pitta, spices, dung,
drains, ground coffee, hidden
jasmine, sweat, insults, shouts,
jingles, brays, the warning of
the porter as he hurtles by with
his cart laden with meat, the
rattle of dice on backgammon
boards and above all the bells
and the recorded cries of the

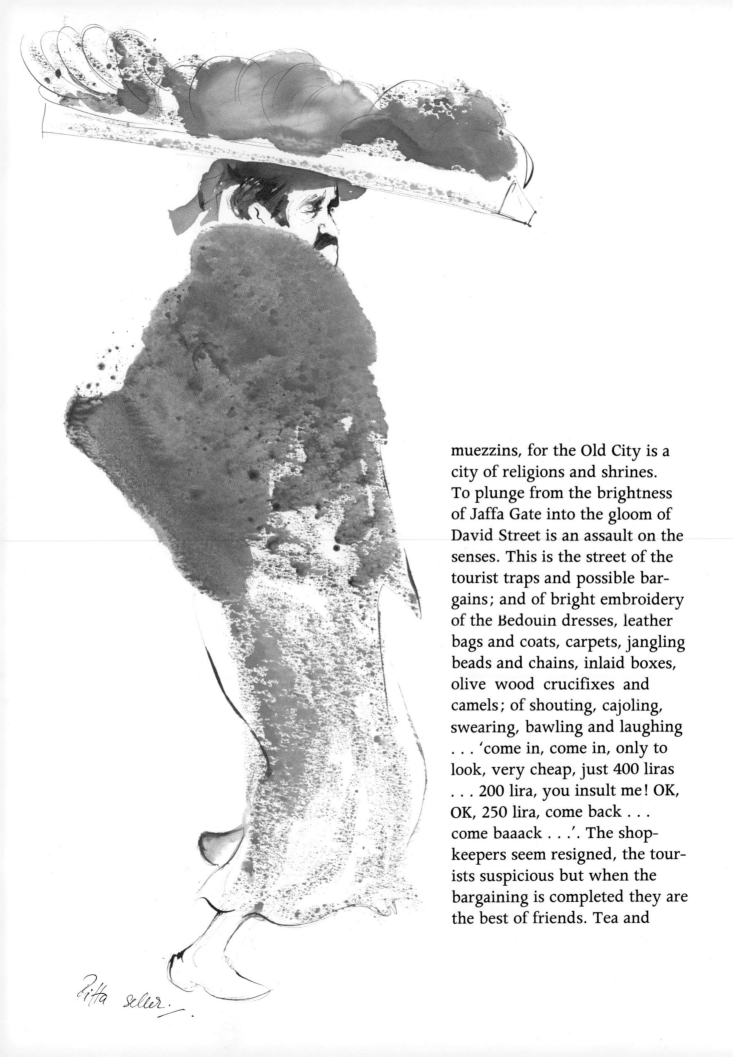
Pitta seller.

muezzins, for the Old City is a
city of religions and shrines.
To plunge from the brightness
of Jaffa Gate into the gloom of
David Street is an assault on the
senses. This is the street of the
tourist traps and possible bargains; and of bright embroidery
of the Bedouin dresses, leather
bags and coats, carpets, jangling
beads and chains, inlaid boxes,
olive wood crucifixes and
camels; of shouting, cajoling,
swearing, bawling and laughing
. . . 'come in, come in, only to
look, very cheap, just 400 liras
. . . 200 lira, you insult me! OK,
OK, 250 lira, come back . . .
come baaack . . .'. The shopkeepers seem resigned, the tourists suspicious but when the
bargaining is completed they are
the best of friends. Tea and

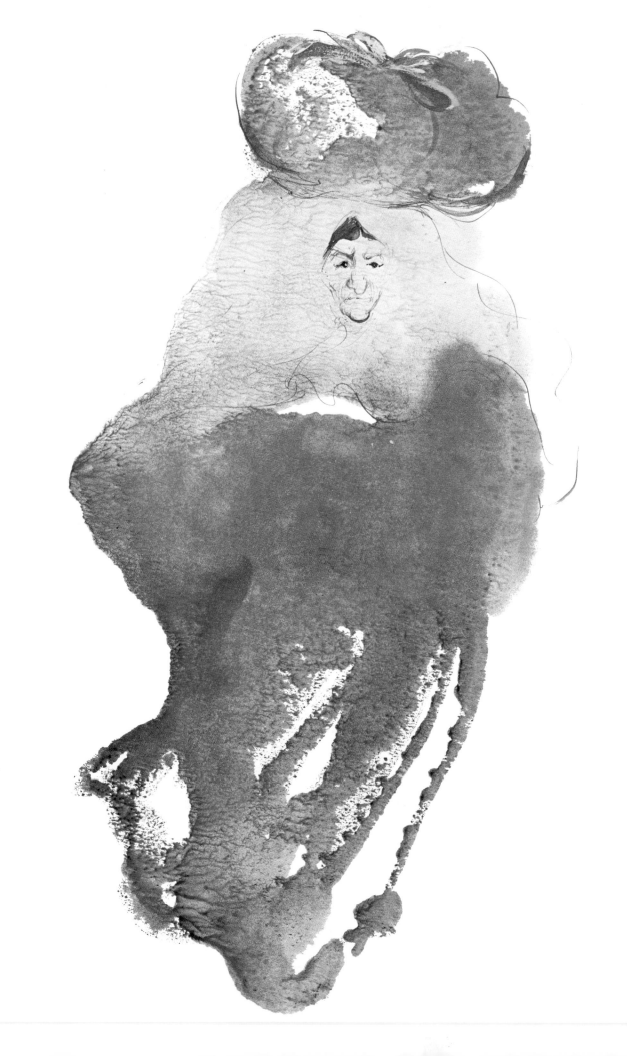

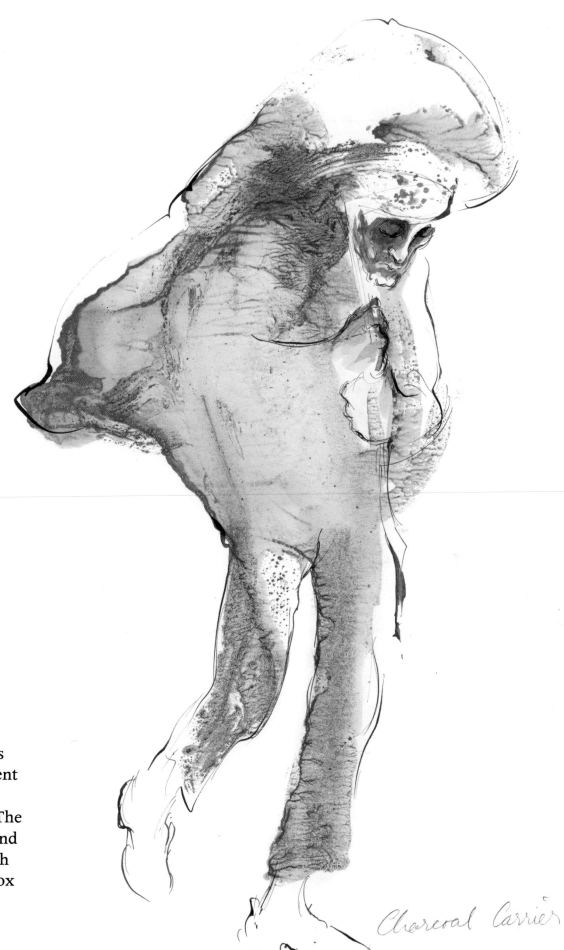

Charcoal Carrier

coffee appear, addresses are
exchanged: 'Tell your friends
about my shop.' It is an ancient
ritual.

The streets are crowded. The
passing masses shove, push and
elbow their way. People touch
more in the Old City, Orthodox

Armenian
Prelate

Jew rubs against Bedouin, Armenian priest against American tourist. There's no choice. It was long ago stipulated by the builders of the narrow passages and covered arcades.

Colour, sound and smell mingle and separate and mix again. The tourists are the peacocks, their Hawaiian flowered shirts and easy-travel yellow

Porter

Hasidic Jew.

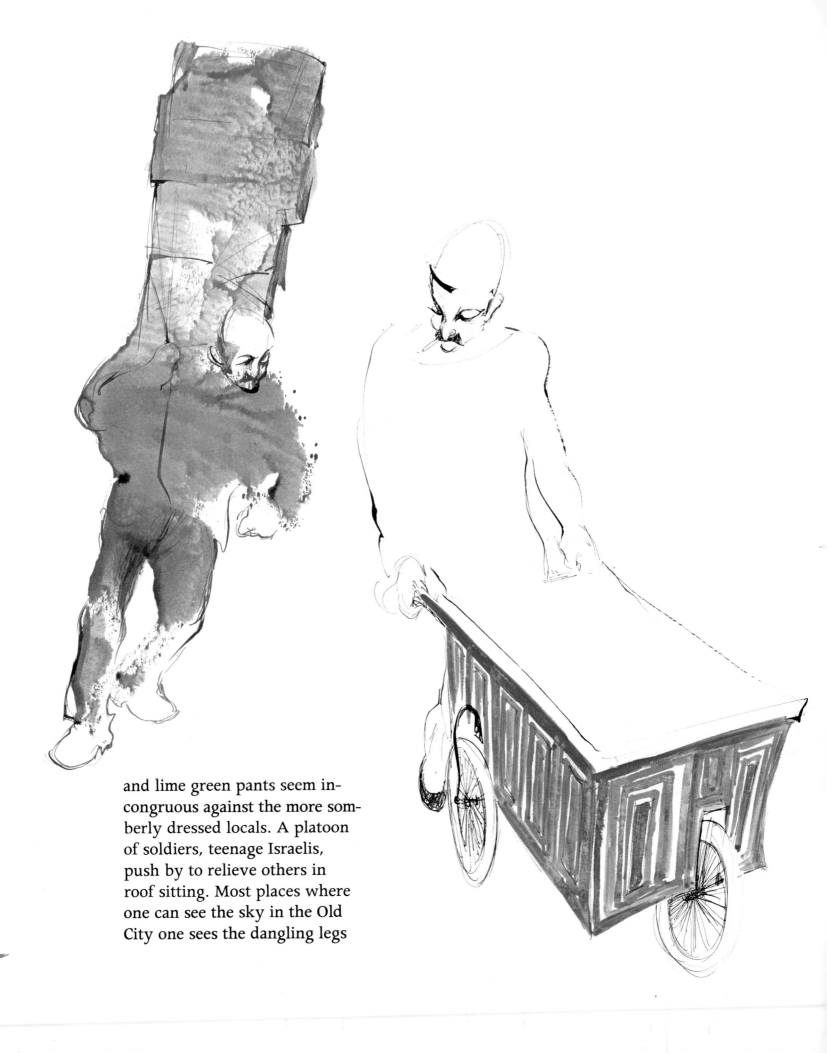

and lime green pants seem in-
congruous against the more som-
berly dressed locals. A platoon
of soldiers, teenage Israelis,
push by to relieve others in
roof sitting. Most places where
one can see the sky in the Old
City one sees the dangling legs

of soldiers; this is the most out-
ward sign that the Old City for
some is occupied territory; the
other signs are more subtle.

Greek
Priests.

Deeper in the souk the tourist shops thin out a little and the more traditional pattern of the Middle Eastern town reasserts itself. A street of butchers interspersed with shashlik sellers, a street of tinsmiths and blacksmiths, a street of dry good stalls, buckets, rope, beans, sponges, spaghetti, chickpeas, material, rice, anything and everything can be bought in the Triple Market. A group of herb and spice sellers down Chain Street, pitta vendors on corners, in a dead end a row of tailors and shoemakers.

سوق الباشورة.

Tailors & Cobblers:
Market Bashora.

TRUFIKWAHB

"Toffee" 1st class guide plus — all languages

They are a happy bunch given to playing practical jokes on each other. One of them scrawled something in Arabic across my drawing to much merriment from the others. In the Straw Market are the basket makers; the domed fruit and vegetable market off David Street has been on the same site for a thousand years. The noise level is higher and the shoppers more serious. The village women strike hard bargains and pile their purchases on their heads. A Greek priest carefully feels the aubergines, cameras click and the women selling parsley and mint near the entrance scream their indignation. An Arab approaches and explains that it is against Islamic law for the women to be photographed.

Tourists move in groups. The leader waves a stick with a scarf attached, the stragglers get chivvied into line:

عبد عاشور
Abet Ashimi.

قياس الأقدام
سليمان و التلبيس
عبد الهاشمي
Abed. Hasheime.

The Happy Tailors & Cobblers of Market Bosttra

Hazan.
customer waiting
for his shoe.

Off David St.
Fruit & Veg.
Market.

'Hurry up, Amy, at twelve
o'clock sharp we go to the Holy
Sepulchre.' For further identi-
fication they wear identical
hats with the name of the different tours printed across the
front.

Hats play a big part in Old
City patterns. Arabs wear kaffi-
yehs, black and white squared;
the younger men prefer the red
and white once the uniform of
Glubb Pasha's Arab Legion, now
symbol of the Palestinians. The
more sophisticated wear red
tarbouches, a legacy of Turkish
days and a sign of a pilgrimage
to Mecca. There is still an old
man in Greek Patriarchate Street
with the brass molds and steam
bath to make the fez. The
Christians have a larger variety

of headgear. Greek priests with black stovepipes, Armenians with the high pointed hood, symbol of their beloved Ararat, the Ethiopians with flatter stovepipes, Copts with round bonnets, Russian nuns with black scarves topped by velvet caps . . .

Orthodox Jews wear round cartwheels, knitted kippahs, or prim porkpies stuck on the back of their heads; each hat a symbol.

Ethiopian nun.

Ethiopian Monk.

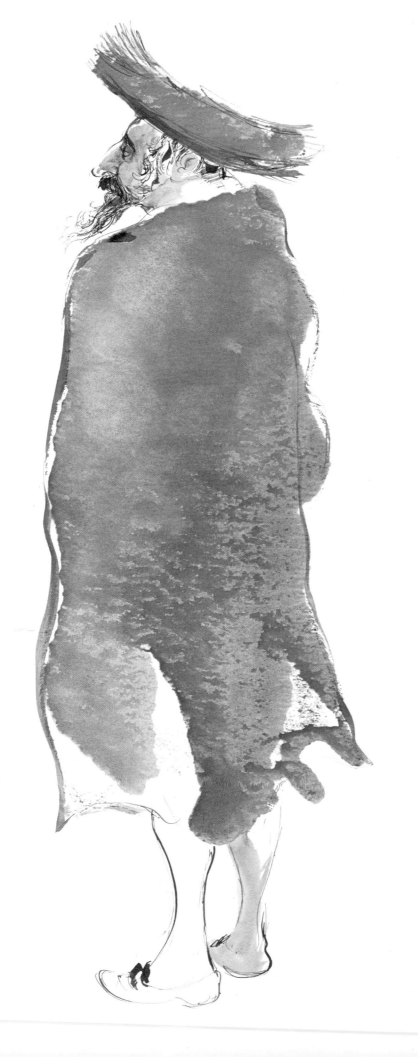

It is easy to get lost in the Old City. There seems no logic behind the crisscrossing alleys, the domed souks, the unexpected squares. But it is easy to get found too. One will always sooner or later come to the medieval walls that Suleiman the Magnificent had built. They are two and a half miles long. Suleiman baptized them by having the two engineers responsible hung. They had made the grave error of forgetting to include Mount Zion within the walls. The walls are being excavated and the successive layers are slowly being revealed; Saracen, Crusader, Byzantine, Herodian even Hasmonean, mute witnesses to the turmoil of Jerusalem's history.

Russian Priests.

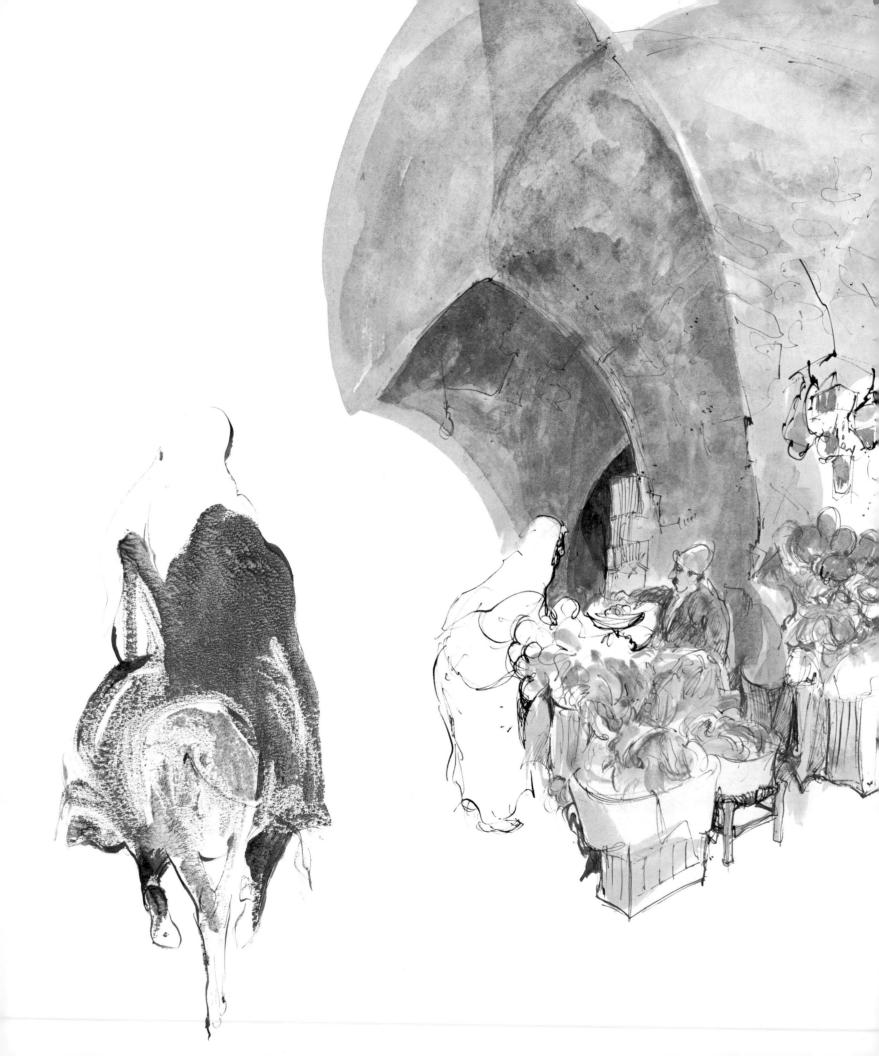

Piercing the walls are eight gates which, with the exception of the Golden Gate walled up by the Turks to prevent the coming of the Messiah, are never closed. From the fifteenth century it was the responsibility of the Sephardi Jews to keep the keys to the gates. Every time a new sultan was appointed they would anoint and bless the keys before returning them to the Turks.

The gates are the mouths of the city. Two of them swallow the bulk of the traffic, two

Fruit Market

legged, four legged and three wheeled; hand pushed carts with a tyre dragging behind acting as the brake.

The Damascus Gate is the most oriental in character and serves the residents of East Jerusalem, the Arab sector, and the villagers who arrive at the bus station aboard the ramshackle buses. The village and Bedouin women position themselves at strategic points just inside the gate and along Al Wad Street to sell bunches of spring onions, lettuces, mint, parsley, dill and bolts of brilliant cloth. They are stout (Arab men do not like thin women, to have one is to indicate one cannot feed her properly) and wear long black and purple dresses brightened across the bosom with vivid embroidery, once all hand sewn now frequently machine made. Once, complained a Palestinian shopowner, one could buy their dresses very cheaply. Now they ask ridiculous prices and the young do not have their grandmother's talent for sewing. An old hand embroidered dress in his shop can cost up to five hundred dollars.

Occasionally one sees Iranian women clad from head to toe in

Entrance
Damascus Gate
outside.

Damascus Gate.

Inside.

Vegetable Seller.

Cloth
Seller
on Al Wad.

floating muslin, patterned with spots and circles.

On the steps leading down to the Damascus Gate are the beggars, heads bowed over horrific infirmities which never seem to heal, hands outstretched. Almsgiving is very much part of the Islamic code. An informal carpet market takes place in one corner, tea and coffee sellers with their brass urns sit outside. To sit an hour reaps many dividends. A runaway mule, a fight between two beggars (each 'owns' a step and no trespassing is allowed), an overturned three wheeler with its load of sugary syrup splashed in the path of the unaware passer-by, Hassidic Jews with bent, mumbling heads taking a short cut from Mea Shearim to the Wailing Wall, and a cacophony of cursing, braying and laughter. It is reminiscent of a Gilray cartoon.

Just inside are the money exchangers, giving they claim the same rate of exchange as the banks. No matter how much one argues one always loses between two and ten percent. The Bedouin women are here, the sweet seller with his smug marmalade cat sitting in the tray at the base of his stand, the old Negro

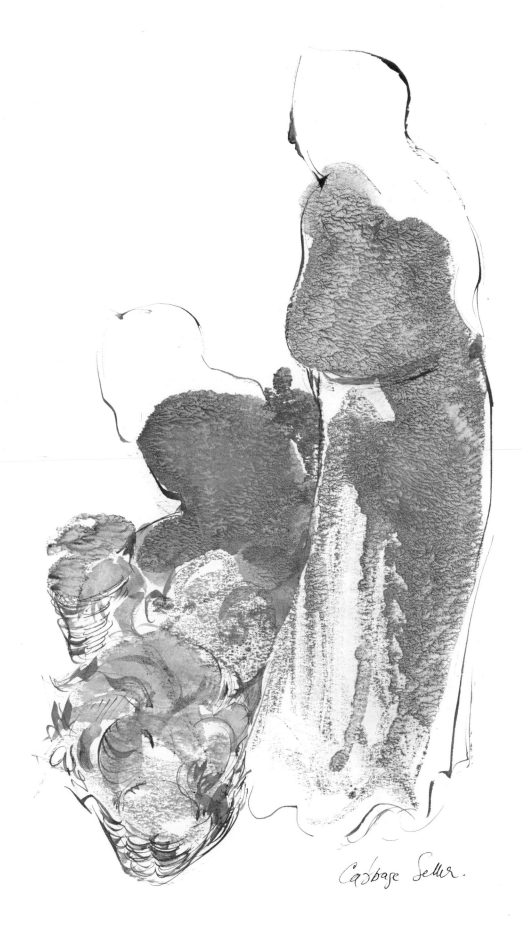

Cabbage Seller.

Tea Seller.
3 pounds a cup of tea.
Aba Sam. Yet halla Johan.

Tea Seller
Singing Bell Tinga lins
a ling a linga ling

who sells yoghurt and cheese,
the newsstand with three month
old *Times* and *Newsweeks* and a
large coffee shop. The coffee
shops are full from dawn to
dusk. Strictly male, they offer
relaxation over Turkish coffee
or mint tea, with arak for the
more daring (though Moslems
in the main do not drink), backgammon and hookahs. To in-
dulge in a hookah needs time.
It is a long ritual to first stuff
the acrid tobacco into the terra-
cotta chimney, then to get it
alight from the piece of glowing
charcoal placed on top. Once
alight it is a peaceful smoke,
best enjoyed with a friend.

Hubbly Bubblers

Omer bin el Khattab St. Just Inside Jaffa Gate

The Jaffa Gate, the other main thoroughfare to the Old City, seems more sophisticated. It is the traditional entrance, and exit, of the many varied conquerors of the city. Romans have marched through its portals (I saw a Roman striding down David Street in tunic, helmet, leather arm and leg gaiters; the effect though was marred by the rucksack on his back). Herod built the Citadel and its three towers, in one of which he imprisoned his wife, Mariamme, for suspected infidelity while he visited Rhodes. Crusaders, and Turks have entered and, more recently, General Allenby who dismounted his horse because, he said, he could not ride over the holy stones. Kaiser Wilhelm II had the moat filled so that he could drive through and it is because of him that cars, trucks and buses can drive in. The trucks disgorge sides of beef and sundry other produce, foam pillows, plastic buckets, cans of food, to name a few essentials of the souks, the buses disgorge the tourists, the camera clicking starts here, and the cars, particularly the large black limousines, disgorge archbishops, an occasional high

Meat Wagon.

Shoe Shiner.

ranking soldier and the odd
patriarch. The larger and sophisticated tourist shops are
here, with the police barracks
around the corner. One finds the
two information centres, the
Municipality's and the Franciscan's filled with backpackers
and itinerant Catholics, the
orange juice stalls and the shoeshine men. They sit on their
haunches in a row left of the
gate. It is a convenient level to
study the passing footwear.
Boot wearers elicit much excite-
ment and rivalry. With my size
13 shoes I cause quite a com-
motion. Once one places one's
foot on the stand one is fair
game. 'Very cheap, only ten
lira', becomes after a second
polish with a silk rag, twenty
lira and before one knows it
one has had the most expensive
shoeshine job in Jerusalem.
I gave one old man my shoes
to polish while I drew him.
They had the full treatment
because the drawing took
some time. I asked him how
much so he smiled and said it
would only cost three hundred
lira. Furious, I railed against
Arabs, the corruption of the
Middle East, of shoeshine men
in particular, said I would tear

up the drawing and he kept
smiling. I gave him twenty lira
and the next day, assailed by
guilt, another twenty. We became the best of friends and I
had free shoeshines for a week.

Outside the gate on the wall
below the citadel the porters
wait for custom. They wear
vivid carpets on their backs,

Sweet Seller.

ABRAHAM.

Dahood

Early Morning Coffee
with the Porters at
Jaffa Gate — Served
by Mohamed. — The
Best coffee I had in
Jerusalem. 5 stars at least.

Porter

baggy pants and the knitted
cap that seems the uniform of
many working-class Arabs.

Ahmed sells them coffee
while they wait. He announces
his presence by clunking two
brass cups together in one hand.
One brass urn holds the coffee,
kept warm by charcoals in the
base, the other holds washing-
up water. He is small, always
smiles, has six children and the
best coffee in Jerusalem. The
porters both appreciate and
need it. They carry the most
enormous loads on their backs
and what is too much even for
them they pile into their crazy
three wheeled chariots to scoot
and skid their way down David
Street to the bazaars.

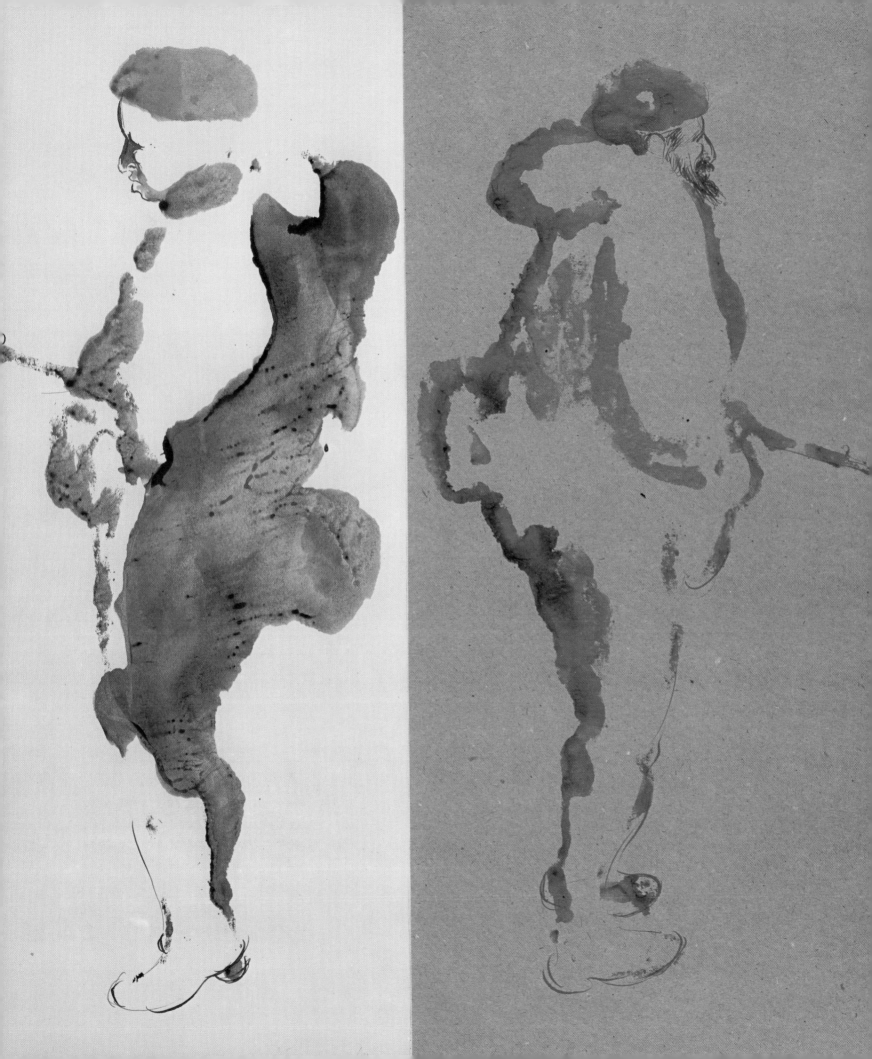

At St Stephen's Gate I met the only camel in the vicinity of the Old City. Saboor and his owner, Salman, give rides to tourists and charge to have their photographs taken. I am exempted and offered a cup of coffee. Cars can infiltrate through

Camel Saboor.
& his master Salman
St Stephens Gate.

Mr Hadji Baba. or FAWZI MANSOUR.

متحف حاجي بابا
القدس
فوزي منصور

St Stephen's Gate but not too far, only to the bottom of the first part of the Via Dolorosa. It was here that the army brought an armoured car during the school children's protest at Jimmy Carter's visit and positioned it outside the best felafel shop in the city. The soldiers ate outside, swinging their truncheons and riot helmets amongst Arabs and tourists.

Down the road Mr Hadji Baba, Jerusalem's answer to Orson Welles is unhappy about the protests and riot gear. It is bad for business. He owns an antique shop packed with Byzantine mosaics, Roman glass, pieces from every stage of Jerusalem's history. Modesty is not one of his shortcomings. 'I have the best antique shop in the Old

City. Twenty five years in business and customers from all over the world.' He continues to grumble about the protests, still what can one do, educate one's children, his son is studying law in England, the rest is up to God and with a shrug he returns to his backgammon game.

In fact it would be impossible for the Via Dolorosa to be empty for any length of time. Every afternoon the Franciscans hold a procession. They stop at each Station of the Cross, chant, pray, and continue their melancholy way to the Holy Sepulchre. On Fridays there is the added symbolism of a devout Catholic bent over with the weight of a wooden cross but somehow the Bermuda shorts of the pseudo-Christ I saw spoilt the effect.

Via Dolorosa

Herod's Gate is narrow and slips sideways into the city. Friday is a big day in the Old City, the Moslem holiday, the start of the Jewish Sabbath. There is a livestock bazaar a little way down from the gate, up against the city's walls. Villagers and Bedouin come to haggle over the price of the forlorn fat-tailed sheep or to peer into the mouth of a scrawny horse; children drag protesting goats, small boys ride donkeys bareback. One offers me a bargain: 'Five camels one dollar.' They are wooden. Muhktars, village headmen, recognizable by the richness and the gold trimming of their robes, saunter from group to group; an imam angrily protests at my attempt to sketch him, the usual noisy human hubbub is overlaid with bleating, mooing and brays.

Of the other gates, New Gate is the latest addition and leads

Sheep Market.
near Herod Gate.
only on Fridays

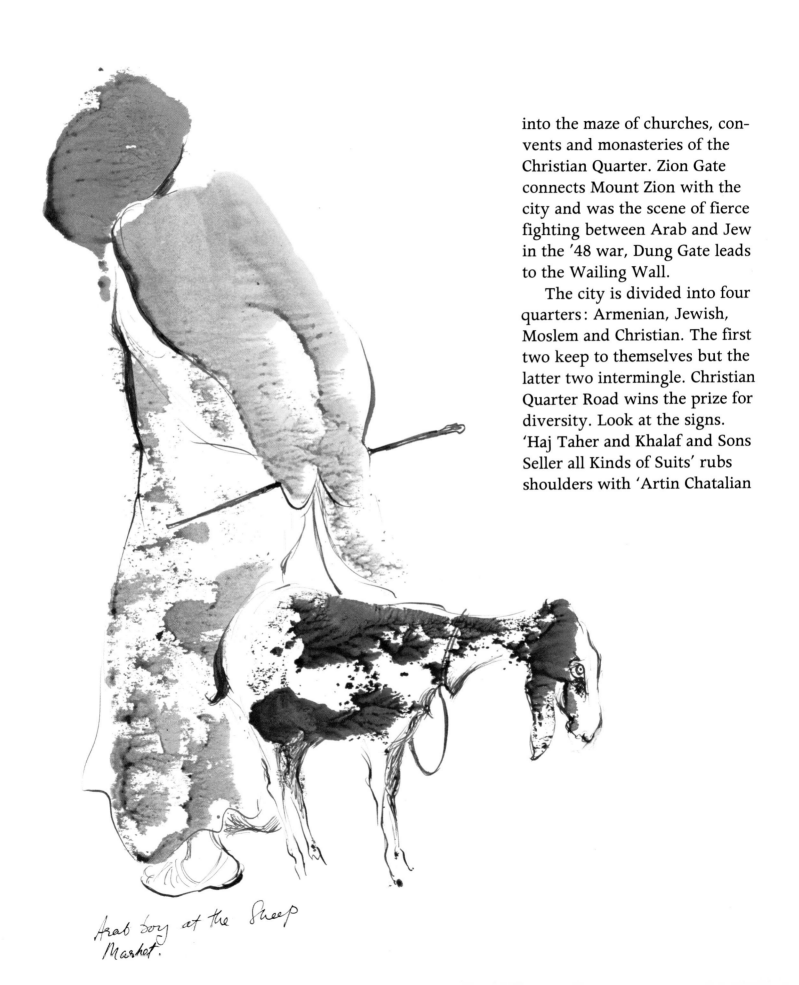

Arab boy at the Sheep
Market.

into the maze of churches, convents and monasteries of the Christian Quarter. Zion Gate connects Mount Zion with the city and was the scene of fierce fighting between Arab and Jew in the '48 war, Dung Gate leads to the Wailing Wall.

The city is divided into four quarters: Armenian, Jewish, Moslem and Christian. The first two keep to themselves but the latter two intermingle. Christian Quarter Road wins the prize for diversity. Look at the signs. 'Haj Taher and Khalaf and Sons Seller all Kinds of Suits' rubs shoulders with 'Artin Chatalian

Shoemaker', 'Acropolis Souvenirs of Antonios Sabat' is opposite 'Gino's Pizzas'. Gino is from Milan. He visited Jerusalem on a pilgrimage many years ago, married a Catholic Arab girl and makes genuine Italian pizzas. 'Jerusalem Arts Museum Konstantinou Lizou' is next door to 'Wadi Razzouk Electric Tattoo Modern Machines Jerusalem'. Wadi Razzouk is a gentle old man whose family have had a monopoly on tattooing in the Old City for generations. For the Christian pilgrims

Sheep Market Herod Gate

Ⲙ|ⲩⲟ|Ⲛ⳿Ⲣ⳾ⲭⲥ
ⲱ|ⲭⲥ|ⲝ

1976

الرب
المسيح المصلوب

Coptic Monk.

Lemonargos.

Michael.
showing his
Tattoos.

Tattoo

a tattoo was the mark of a completed pilgrimage and a sign of
prestige. It is not so fashionable
nowadays save for the Bedouin
women, whose faces are frequently covered in blue tattoos,
marks of tribal distinction. Wadi
has almost retired and prefers
to sit in his friend's barber shop.
He is a Coptic Orthodox and is
sad that his son does not follow
the family work. At the moment
it is maintained only by his
younger brother. He offers me a
coffee and tells me that he never
takes his astrakhan hat off (he's
completely bald, says the barber
with a wink), except to change
it in summer for a fez.

One of my favourite places to
sit was in front of a coffee shop
and tourist boutique belonging
to a family of five Palestinian
brothers just outside the Holy
Sepulchre. They were relentless
in their pursuit of characters
for me to draw. They cornered
a Coptic monk, a Franciscan
friar, an American tourist, two
Moslem brothers, a small Arab

WADI RAZZOUK

Electric Tattoo.

WITH ELECTRIC MODERN
MACHINES

Wadi Razzouk   Tattooist

not Shuref SHANA !!!!!

Tawfe Whab (Toffee
Guide.)
Greek Orthodox Arab.
Born in Jerusalem.
in 1913.

Artin.
Sissegian... uphwrini
Armenian guide

girl, a young Israeli, and when the streets emptied they brought over their neighbours. I drew Mr Hijazy, leather goods in the Muristan, who has been on a *haj* to Mecca and has walked around the Kaa'aba seven times, and Mr Dakkak and his son, owners of a large religious shop full of rosaries and crucifixes. They spoke precise English and the old man reminisced of the good old days under the British Mandate.

I drew Abraham, the Catholic Kawass, Galil the flower seller,

Rafi: Rozenas.

Student studying
tourism
סטודנט לומד
Hebrew ↑
תיירות
Israeli.

outside entrance
to the
HOLY SEPULCHRE.
Sunday Morning —

20 Postcards for a Dollar.

Two Brothers Omran & Johan (bottom) Omran works for
the Catholic Church (Franciscan).
Johan sells postcards on Sunday. — the rest of the time
works in a Garage on V.Ws:

Johan → جواد الله   عمر ان الله ← Omran.

ابراهيم السعدي

Ibrahim Assoli

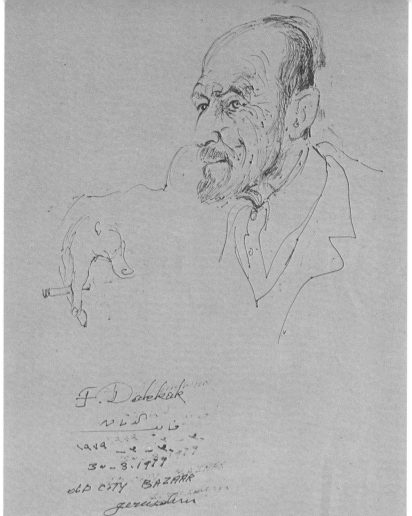

F. Dalekak
فلان بكلان
١٩٧٩ - ٣ - ٣٠
30 - 3 . 1979
OLD CITY BAZAAR
jerusalem

Mr. Honey.
Guide.

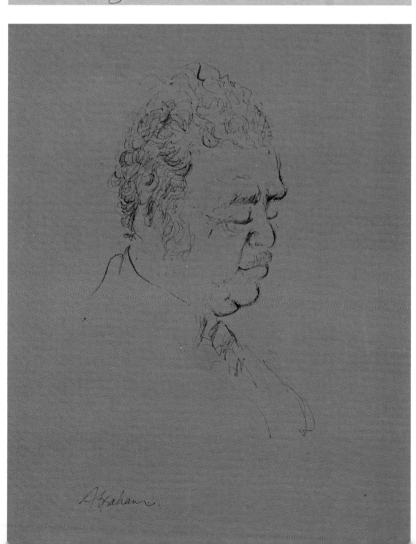

Abraham.

Galil. Abraham
Flower Seller.

the Holy Sepulchre in search of business. There is Mr Honey, Tawfe, who with the approach of Orthodox Palm Sunday supplements his income by making intricate structures of palm leaves, Abraham, one of whose

who pretends he is only delivering flowers not selling them: 'They can't catch me that way.' He is philosophical about the situation and has learnt Hebrew. Not so the youngest of the five brothers. He is vehement in his belief that the only solution is a Palestinian State, that too much bitterness has passed between Jew and Arab for them ever to live peacefully together. Anyway he says, he's off to the States soon to pursue his studies in chemistry.

The guides congregate at the coffee shop. Occasionally they wander about the courtyard of

طلال زهير حجازي
القدس الشريف
"Eastern Leather Work
Exhibition"

Zuhair Hijazy

"Sweet Joseph"

J. Kaplarian

ears was bitten off in a fight, and Artin, a dapper Armenian. Armenians are everywhere in the Old City. Opposite is the barber shop of Sweet Joseph who fled Armenia fifty years ago. He's retired really, sixty year's work is enough, but likes to come to his shop to see his friends even though, he winks, he has such a young wife at home. He is a large old man and furious with himself at the moment as he slipped in his bath and broke his hip. They fixed it with a silver pin which is a small compensation. Rafi is a young Armenian who has returned from six years in Europe and opened a T-shirt boutique in the Muristan. He was born in Jerusalem where his father was a tailor and Rafi was to follow in father's footsteps, hence the European tour. He was supposed to study fashion design but spent more time selling football tickets. Tailoring is too much like hard work, morning until night, while putting transfers on T-shirts is easy, no sweat. His shop seems to be a meeting place. Youngsters drift in and out, Arab, Armenian, Greek and three young Copts whose grandfathers came

from Egypt to settle in Jerusalem. They can neither write nor read Coptic, all their study is done in Arabic.

Just off the Via Dolorosa is Stephan's tile shop. Unlike Rafi, he is following in the family tradition. His father was brought from Armenia to repair the tiles on the Dome of the Rock at the

Amin-RAGA-NASSAR
أمين رجا نصار
Coptic.

GUS
George Elias
أليا ج ١٥ ج

Ousama RaJa NaSSar
أسامة رجا نصار

Rex Studio

Mr. Rex. landed at
Mont Ararat. with a Boat.
Photographer. from the time of Noah.

beginning of the British Mandate. Then the second wave of massacres in Armenia took place and the Turks, claiming that there had never been Armenian tilemakers, sent over Turks and his father never completed the job. Stephan eventually opened his own tile business and is responsible for all the tile street signs in the Old City. After the reunification of the city in 1967, Stephan was asked to add Hebrew to the signs. The kiln is next door supervised by his brother; Stephan is the designer, borrowing from many different sources, Byzantine, Armenian, Arabic motifs and old Crusader maps.

Photography is another traditional Armenian occupation. Mr Rex (I never discovered his true name), claims he landed by boat on Mount Ararat and has been a photographer since the time of Noah. He looks like Chamberlain and purposely carries an umbrella to heighten the effect. Though I could rarely fathom what he was saying, he is obviously much in demand. The walls of his small shop are covered with photographs of

Stephen Karakashian & Bros
Tile Maker & Seller

THE JERUSALEM FRUIT EXCHANGE (OLD)
معرض القدس القديمة للخضار والفواكه

Patriarchs, Archbishops, ban-
quets, weddings, and even Jordanian soldiers and British
officers.

More articulate is the Armenian baker. He opens twice a
week, Wednesdays and Saturdays, to make special Armenian
pizzas, highly seasoned ground
meat on a thin dough. Why
twice a week? He shrugs. Why
work more than one has to? The
tax department didn't believe
him until an Israeli newspaper
wrote an article about his bakery.
Now he shows the cutting to
any disbelieving tax officials.
His grandfather made pizzas in
Turkey eighty years ago and
his father was the official baker
of the Armenian Compound.
The present baker used to be

Zagaria's
shop
→

Heart of Triple Market

Էսեր Մնեշեան
Nver Meneshian
&
Jack Meneshian. The Armenian Community Bakery
opened twice a week Wednesdays & Saturdays.

the sports teacher for the Armenian school but now he is back
to baking. His father retired to
Los Angeles, and he himself
lived there for a while, but his
wife was homesick so they returned to Jerusalem.

Armenian pizzas, Italian
pizzas, there are even Arab
pizzas. Muhammed Ali, 'the
baker not the boxer', makes
special order house bread and
pizzas helped by innumerable
small children. An egg, some
cheese and salt broken into a
piece of bread dough, it is the
cheapest meal in town, a fact
well known by the backpacking
brigade.

Mohammed Ali,
da Baker
not Boxer

His Assistant.
making Pizzas

child carrying bread

From the roof of
the Ecce Homo Convent.
Before lunch.

Perhaps the best place to get an overall idea of the Old City is to climb to the top of the 'Ecce Homo' Convent, home of the Sisters of Zion, members of the Dominican Order. One can see most of the walls, and beyond them the walls and buildings of new Jerusalem, to the other side the Mount of Olives, the Garden of Gethsemane, the Wilderness of Judea. In the foreground is the golden dome of the Dome of the Rock, the black dome of the Church of our Lady of the Spasm and a graceful Mameluke minaret; further away, the new arches and buildings of the Jewish Quarter with the spires of the Armenian Compound behind, and every-

where a cobweb of television aerials, lines of washing, interspersed with crosses, crescents, cupolas . . . . One gets a small idea of the many symbols, dogmas, nationalities, groups secular and religious, that have gone into the composition of this complicated city.

Another view from the Ecce Homo Convent. — after lunch

A soldier showed the way as Mount Zion was very dark. He peered into a long room below the Greek Seminary: 'They must be at David's Tomb.' They were.

The seats are arranged in a semi-circle; unmarried girls one side, unmarried men the other, married couples the buffer in the middle. Facing the audience is a drummer, a pianist and two guitarists. The words on the drum read 'Diaspora Yeshiva Band'. A banner below says the same in English and Hebrew.

The musicians resemble hillbillies, or rather my idea of a hillbilly come to town on a Sunday. They wear shiny black suits and brimmed black hats, except for the drummer who wears a kippah. Each is heavily bearded.

The audience is quiet, the setting serene. We are in a small square outside David's Tomb surrounded by walls and a large cypress tree. There's a period of testing, a few coughs . . . . 'THERE'S A GOD IN THE WORLD'.

'Somebody is running the show . . .' The guitarist bellows through his microphone.

'Ah one, ah two, ah three.'

Saturday night at the Diaspora Yeshiva.

There's a God in the World
Somebody is running the"
Show - !

שירה ערב
בערב 9:00 אנטרנשענל מיוזיק

Crash, thump the band is off with a solid, throbbing beat.

The soldier leaps to his feet and a boy with sidelocks from the unmarried male side joins him. They hold hands, jump and twist in a circle; it's the traditional Hassidic dance, the hora. With not even a drink they try to outdo the band, catching every note with their gyrating bodies. Even after the music has stopped they continue to hop and jump. Then they stop abruptly, wipe the sweat from their brows and return to their seats.

How sweet it is
all Jewish Brothers
together.

Saturday Night with the Diaspora Yeshiva.

'There was a great rabbi,' it's the guitarist again, 'who said foolish people try to solve their problems in every way but the right way, like a dog. Beat it with a stick and it'll bite

the stick not the beater. So don't
be a dog, beat about right to the
core. And where's that? You
know, I know, but sometimes
we prefer to be dogs.'

More music, more dances, more dancers. Arms entwined around necks, high kicks and jumps but always the same dance and never female dancers. Songs: 'How sweet it is all Jewish brothers together . . .' Homilies: 'There was a kid who prayed to God for a bike. His father laughed at him. "What, do you expect God to make a miracle and give you a bike?" But that kid prayed on and after a few days the father asked, "Where is the bike?" "It's not here yet." "What did God say?" "Later," said the boy. That's hope. Like us. We've been wandering around praying and hoping for 2,000 years. Next year in Jerusalem. Next year. And it happened, that miracle happened, right here. We are in JERUSALEM! God promised he would bring us back. It's like Superman, Spiderman!'

The Wailing Wall

Thump, crash and the music spirals off again. Have I stumbled into a Hassidic Baptist meeting?

'This spot is a very special spot for us Jews. A lot of you have it too easy. When you want to pray you just go right up to the Wall and pray. It wasn't always like that. For twenty years until 1967 Jews from all

over came here because it was the only place from the top of that minaret
where one could see the Wall. That friends was at a time when you as a
Jew could not worship at your holiest place . . . . Let's all make our
little peace in the world. Take your right hand and raise it, now the left,
and let's all clap hard . . . .'

The music crashes on again.

Shabtai had provided the introduction to the Diaspora Yeshiva Band's
Saturday evening get-together.

The Diaspora Yeshiva was in another part of Mount Zion and I had
wandered in by chance and sat next to Shabtai. Yeshiva literally means

Shabtai
Herman

ב"ה

ושיבת הגולה ע"י
שבתי הרמן ציור
וישי הגלות צייר זה ציין בגיל 3'13 קבל מלך זבל
אלף הגולים

At the Diaspora Yeshiva

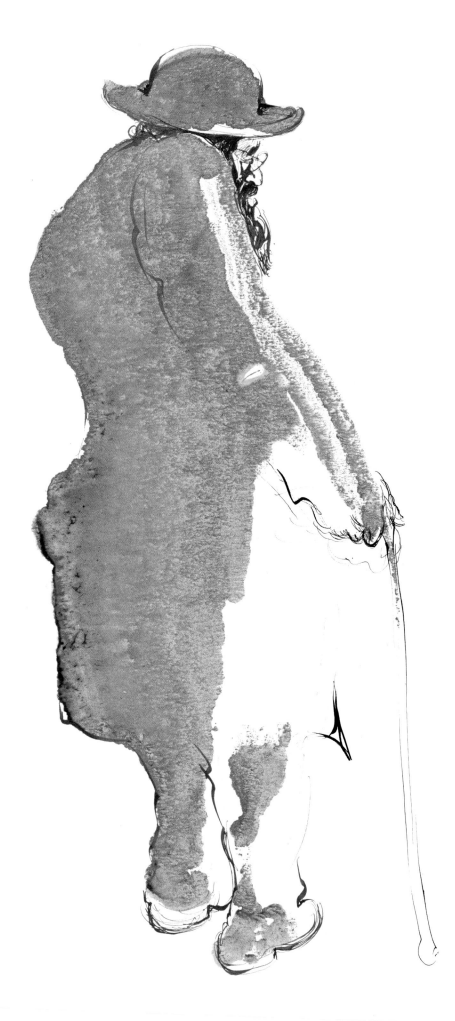

'to sit' and it is where religious
Jews study and discuss Judaic
scriptures and writing together.
That morning the discussion
was on the word 'pure' in rela-
tion to oil for the lamps of the

Temple destroyed so many years ago. A lively and sometimes heated debate continued for an hour until the meeting broke up.

Shabtai invited me to his home in the Jewish Quarter. The wealthy citizens and priests in Herod's time lived here, reaching the Temple by a bridge that spanned the Cheesemaker's Valley. It was razed by the Romans during the Jewish Revolts but was slowly built up again until by Turkish times 20,000 or so Jews lived here. This quarter was the scene in 1948 of a siege that lasted several months. Separated from Jewish Jerusalem by Arab troops, with little food and water it was held by a handful of the Haganah, the Jewish defence corps, while the rabbis and yeshiva students continued their studies. Finally, with half the quarter bombed, two rabbis, despite protests from the Haganah, raised the white flag and the one thousand odd inhabitants were granted safe passage to Western Jerusalem by the Arab Legion. The few remaining Haganah were taken prisoners. Many of the old rabbis had not left the Quarter for decades. One, a hundred years old, had last seen modern

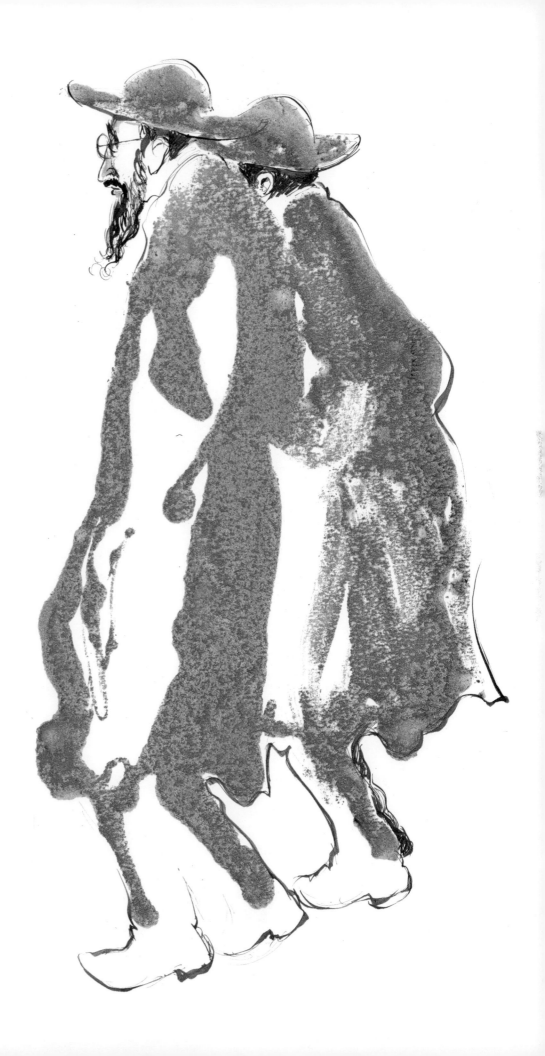

ARARAT RD.

YISHUV COURT MUSEUM

EL ARMAN RD

Boundary of Armenian Quarter & Jewish Quarter

Jerusalem ninety years before. Arabs moved into what houses were left standing but the pendulum keeps swinging and the Israelis regained the Old City in 1967. The rebuilding of the Jewish Quarter started then and still goes on. Compared with the rest of the Old City it has an odd, antiseptic feeling. The finished streets and buildings are spotless, there are no crowds, little noise and the few shops are chic boutiques and small art galleries. One belongs to Eliahu Schwartz. He works

I extend my hand to shake hers, but with no response, withdraw it again. Shabtai sheepishly explains that it is against religious law for a married woman to touch a strange man. He can only touch her on special occasions.

The house is quite empty, they have only been married six weeks, and it has the traditional vaulted ceilings and thick walls. The new houses in the Jewish Quarter are designed to resemble the old style as much as possible. Shabtai is a member of the Diaspora Yeshiva which will support him for the rest of his life from funds mostly raised in the USA. He says it is less Orthodox than other yeshivas in the Old City, it has the band for instance. Many of its members were formerly hippies and drifters, the majority Americans with a few French and English. There are hardly any Israelis. In the yeshiva, besides the study of the Judaic scriptures, they are taught ritual animal slaughter, scribal arts and circumcision

After serving tea, Julie continues to work. It is midday Friday and the Sabbath begins at dusk when the first star appears in the evening sky.

and sells but doesn't live here: 'Its too closed, all walls and no gardens.' The quarter is still very new and more and more people are slowly moving in.

Shabtai and his wife Julie are newly married. He is from South Africa, she from America.

July Herman
from Indiana
married

Shabtai Herman
from Cape Town S.A.
a Student at
a Yeshiva (means to sit
& study)

lives in the Jewish
Quarter

Phylactery of the Head

Kippa

Talis

Phylactery of the arm

For the Orthodox, nothing that could be termed as creative—carrying money in your pocket, cooking, cleaning, taking an automatic elevator, turning on a light or driving can be done until Saturday night. Julie is looking through beans for insects. Bugs aren't kosher. She will prepare a dish called cholent of different types of beans, potatoes, eggs, chicken that will simmer all Friday night to be eaten midday Saturday.

I ask Shabtai if I can draw him in his prayer robes. He assents and brings his Talmud, the writings of Rashin, the two phylactergies, one on his head, the other under his arm with a leather strap wound seven times around, the prayer shawl and the scarf around his waist. Once settled he tells me we can talk while he studies but about nothing impure, like how the football season went, for example. He returned to the passage that had been studied at the yeshiva that morning. For an hour he read and discussed with Julie and me the meaning behind the word 'pure'. He will be a student all his life and there is no sense of urgency in his study. He has time and books, hundreds of them. I asked him why he came to Jerusalem. He took me to the roof of his house: 'Jerusalem is God's city. Miracles happen here.' He explained that a group of fellow students had prayed for rain as it had been a very dry winter, and after the prayers it poured for a week. A miracle! A few days earlier an Arab had told me he was responsible for the rain. He too had prayed very hard.

There are not many Jews who actually live in the Old City. Those that are in the Jewish Quarter are mostly religious and connected with the several yeshivas and synagogues. For the more secular this raises problems. One family was not spoken to by their religious neighbours for several months because the wife had taken her washing down on a Sabbath.

Though they might not live here the Jews are a constant thread in the tapestry of the Old City. It is their symbol, it houses their most religious shrine, the remnant of Solomon's Temple, the Wailing Wall. Only twice in the two thousand year old history of Jewish presence in Jerusalem have they been denied access, during Crusader times and for the twenty years under Jordanian rule. Now, day and night, there is always someone praying there. Little pieces of paper stick out between the cracks in the wall, prayers and requests from those in need. The area immediately

behind the wall was cleared
after 1967 and its Arab inhabitants housed elsewhere. Now it
is a wide expanse of paving
guarded by members of the
Home Guard.

Guard at Entrance
to Wailing Wall

I shall never forget a cocktail party in Jerusalem and my elegant hostess suddenly looking at her watch and saying, 'My Goodness, I shall be late for my guard duty'. Once a week she patrols the streets of Jerusalem or some other duty. The Home Guard is on a voluntary basis but every Israeli does a three year military service, two years for girls. After that, until the age of fifty-five, they do a six week training course each year.

Every day of the week and particularly on the Sabbath there is a constant flow of Hassidic Jews through the Jaffa and Damascus Gates. The men bearded, sidelocked, some wearing fur hats, others broad brimmed homburgs, prayer shawls under long waisted black coats, or in warmer weather, striped silver and white or golden robes with black stockings. Their heads are bowed for fear of seeing some impure sight, a woman in shorts maybe or a couple holding hands. Their women are soberly dressed with wigs covering their bald heads (bald so that they may appear unattractive to other men); the sallow boys have crew cuts but with the ubiquitous sidelocks and kippahs on the backs of their heads. These are the ultra Orthodox who live in Mea Shearim outside the walls.

Each hat, each dress is significant to whatever religious grouping they belong to and has changed little since the sixteenth and seventeenth centuries. In Poland and Russia fur hats would make sense but under a hot Jerusalem sun they look uncomfortable. But they stick to their ancient customs and studies. They are the ones that believe that if every Jew in the world strictly observed the Sabbath rituals the Messiah would come.

There is even a group who refuse to accept the State of Israel. They believe that a country for the Israelites can only be created by God. Under this reasoning David Ben-Gurion's hard won state is an abomination.

The Sabbath brings not only the Orthodox to the Old City. The streets are full of young and old from all over Israel, sightseeing and shopping on their one free day a week, drawn to the very core of the meaning of being Jewish. 'Next year in Jerusalem!' is now a reality.

There are Jews from seventy different countries in Israel, speaking an equivalent number of languages. There are Ashkenazis from West and East Europe, Sephardis from Spain and North Africa, Orientals from Yemen, Iraq and other Eastern countries as far as India. From the time

of the first diaspora under the
Babylonians they have slowly
returned. A small-cross section
can be seen in the Old City each
Sabbath.
The clothes may be uniform,

Joseph

Hussein

Avir.

Black Muslim
Children.

Amed.

The Black Muslims

blue jeans are *de rigeur* with the young, but their faces reflect the many different nationalities that make up the Jewish population.

A few yards from Prison Gate away from Temple Mount are two recessed arches that face each other on either side of the street. During Turkish times one arch led to the Military Headquarters the other to the prison. When I passed it wasn't soldiers or prison guards who sat on the stone benches under the arches but an old man in a shapeless coat. Under the other arch were two gossiping women. Around them played children of various sizes. Their features were negroid and their skin black. It is here in the old prison that the black Moslems live. They are the descendants of Africans brought by the Mameluke rulers in the late thirteenth century from Chad, Senegal, Nigeria and Sudan to guard the gates to the Moslem shrines. No Jews or Christians were allowed on Temple Mount. In the nineteenth century this ruling was relaxed and the Turks permitted various distinguished visitors to tour the shrines. On one occasion the zealous guards had to be locked in the prison for fear they would injure the Christians. They voiced their indignation by howling.

Jibree.

coffee – Dagwa

African Welfare
Club
Prison Gate
Jerusalem

Inside the Black Muslim House
Ahmed's Uncle. Mohamed awa Toxi.

Hussein elected to be my guide. He was fourteen, serious and spoke good English learnt in school. He told me there are thirty families, some two hundred people, who live here sharing the meagre facilities. That the building over there is the African League Youth Centre, where each Saturday they play music and games. Joseph is the best musician, he speaks English but he is shy. That he, Hussein, likes to play football and wants to go to university. That the old man sitting under the arch is his grandfather from Chad, the little girl whose shoelace he is tying his sister. It would seem that some African Moslems on their way back from Mecca frequently decide to stay with the commune and not to return home. This is one explanation of how the community has retained its African characteristics despite intermarriage with local Moslems.

It was difficult to get an overall view of the old prison, it seemed a hotchpotch of shacks with corrugated iron roofs, so Hussein took me to a nearby house for a better view. A mistake. The women yelled at us for invading their privacy. An Arab guard from Prison Gate arrived and I tried to explain I only wanted to make a quick drawing of the prison. To no avail; we were escorted down the steps, Hussein in tears.

He recovered and introduced me to Ahmed. Ahmed was very thin, swayed slightly and had large red-rimmed mournful eyes. He politely invited me to meet his mother. We passed the communal wash house where two large women were immersed in suds and clothes, and the small mosque where on Fridays the men gather to cook a meal and discuss the commune's affairs. Ahmed's house was immaculate in contrast to the dirt and dust outside. An Arabian Night's effect was achieved by the total wallpapering of the walls and vaulted ceiling in various clashing patterns; tartans, orange stripes and swirls. Ahmed's mother, a stately woman with more European features than her son, offered coffee. I attempted conversation with Ahmed's uncle who sat, clothed despite the heat in a sweater, a woollen dressing gown and a woollen cap on his head, on the bed. He told me Ahmed's father was dead, Ahmed was ill which explained the thinness and deformed hands, he himself was not well, they had lived here all their lives. Desultry conversation due to the language barrier but there was an overall togetherness, protectiveness towards Ahmed, pride in his only brother whose

Ne had Kazzaz.

50 Years a guide at the Temple Mount.
During the Second world war with the 24 & 17 Brigade.
South African Forces. in charge of Water & Security.

محمد احمد القزاز   his name in Arabic

Life is very well Thanks God

Dome of the Rock

photograph I was shown; a tightknit family living in one room full of beds, a small table, a cupboard, photographs and a television set.

'Stop, open your bag please.'

'Sorry, madam, you must wear more clothes.' An old man promptly produces, for a small price, a cross between an apron and a shawl to cover the offending bare flesh.

'No holding hands. This a holy place.'

The guards at the Temple Mount are Arabs now. Their task no longer to stop infidels from entering but to make sure that they are decently clad, that they behave respectfully and to search for bombs or firearms, a common enough ritual in Jerusalem.

The Temple Mount, Mount Moriah, Haram Esh Sharif is equally important to all three religions. The Christians claim that Jesus returned here in triumph after the Resurrection and that one can see his throne; for the Moslems it is where Mohammed flew one night from Mecca on Al Buraq, his famous horse, ascended to Heaven to receive revelation from God, and came back down in time

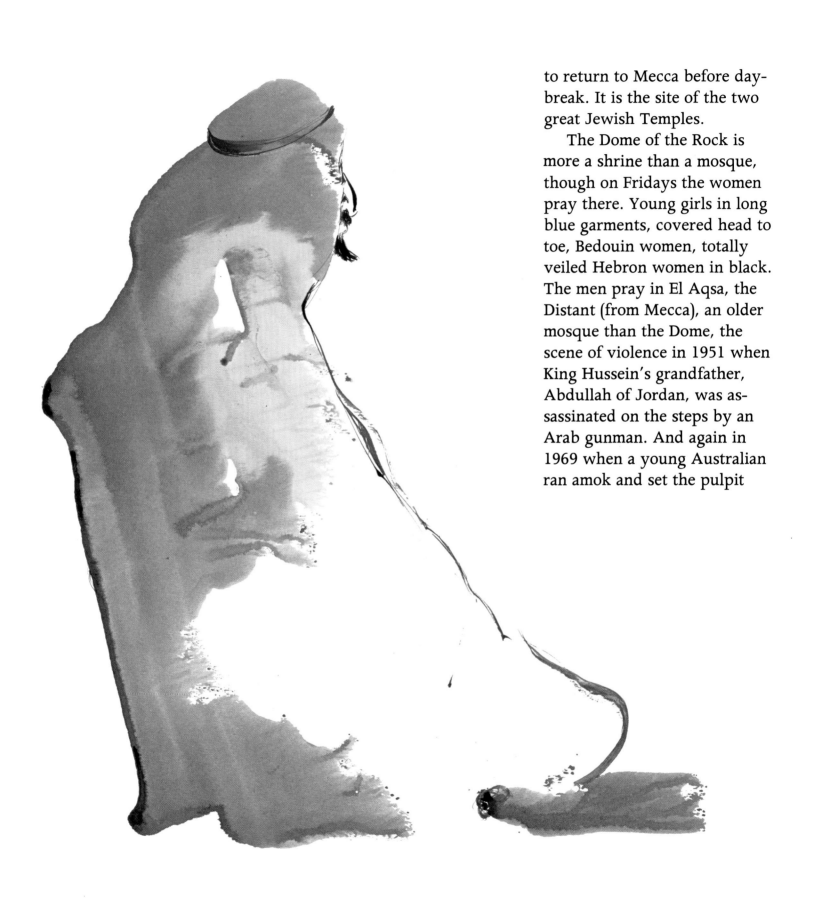

to return to Mecca before day-break. It is the site of the two great Jewish Temples.

The Dome of the Rock is more a shrine than a mosque, though on Fridays the women pray there. Young girls in long blue garments, covered head to toe, Bedouin women, totally veiled Hebron women in black. The men pray in El Aqsa, the Distant (from Mecca), an older mosque than the Dome, the scene of violence in 1951 when King Hussein's grandfather, Abdullah of Jordan, was assassinated on the steps by an Arab gunman. And again in 1969 when a young Australian ran amok and set the pulpit

alight, as well as the southern part of the mosque. Repairs are still going on. Outside is the fountain where the Moslems wash their feet before entering. The guides sit here waiting to show tourists the different shrines or if they can persuade them the whole city. Here I met Nehad who has been a guide for fifty years. During the Second World War he was in Egypt with the South Africans. He says he was in charge of water and security. He enjoyed those years but life now is very well, thanks to God.

To obtain permission to draw inside the mosque I had to visit the Chief of the Moslem Council in his office at Prison Gate. He was puzzled by my request.

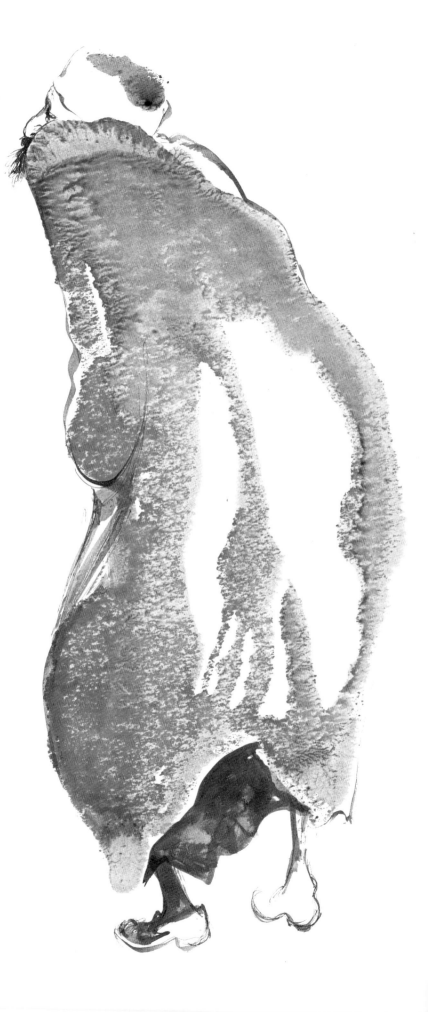

'There are prayers five times
a day in the mosques. You cannot be inside during these times.
Can you make drawings so
quickly in two hours?' I
assured him I could. He shrugged
and signed a small piece of paper
in elegant Arabic script.

The outside of the Dome of
the Rock is spectacular enough;
the golden dome, turquoise
Persian tiles, the bronze doors.
Inside it is stunning; cool and
peaceful despite the intricacy
of the pillars and decorations,
a contrast to the raw slab of
stone in the centre protected
by a wooden fence. It is the
mainspring for many legends in
Judaic and Islamic lore. On it
Abraham offered Isaac for sacrifice and Mohammed headed for
Heaven. David bought it from
the Jebusites, Solomon built
the first altar on top of it. Many

Arab washing feet at
El Aqsa - Mosque

Judaic and Islamic beliefs and
rituals are similar. They both
claim lineage through Abraham,
the Jews through Isaac, the
Arabs through Ishmael (they
believe he was offered for sacrifice on another famous rock,
the Kaa'aba at Mecca). They also
share many of their prophets;
Solomon is particularly revered

Mosaic.
not touched
since 691 A.D.
1187 AD to Saladin
Columns

الحرم الشريف

by both. Neither religion permits portrayal of the human form, neither eats pork, animals must be ritually slaughtered, the Moslems say that the Jews, and the Christians for that matter, are People of the Book and are free to follow their own creeds (Christ is regarded as a kind of minor prophet).

The Moslems in Jerusalem are Sunnis, or Traditionalists, and one cannot help but be

Inside Dome of the Rock.

Special pass for drawing inside the Rock

Amin & Mohamed.
Guards of the Dome of the Rock

Full name
Mohamed abdel qorat Fellad

impressed by the refreshing lack
of ceremony in their religion.
Wherever they are the religious
unfold their prayer rugs and
pray towards Mecca five times
a day. In the mosques there is a
feeling of serenity and acceptance of God, no fuss made. 'God
willing' was the byword of any
religious Arab I talked to, and

for that matter of any Orthodox
Jew. Acceptance, no questions
asked.

I return to the Chain Gate to
draw the policemen. They are
delighted. The bag searching
becomes perfunctory as Ali
from the Mount of Olives poses,
then Ahmed from Bethlehem.
The sergeant arrives. He is
Jewish from North Africa. They
all speak Arabic and Hebrew
and there is an easy camaraderie
amongst them. There are more
than two hundred Arab police
in Jerusalem.

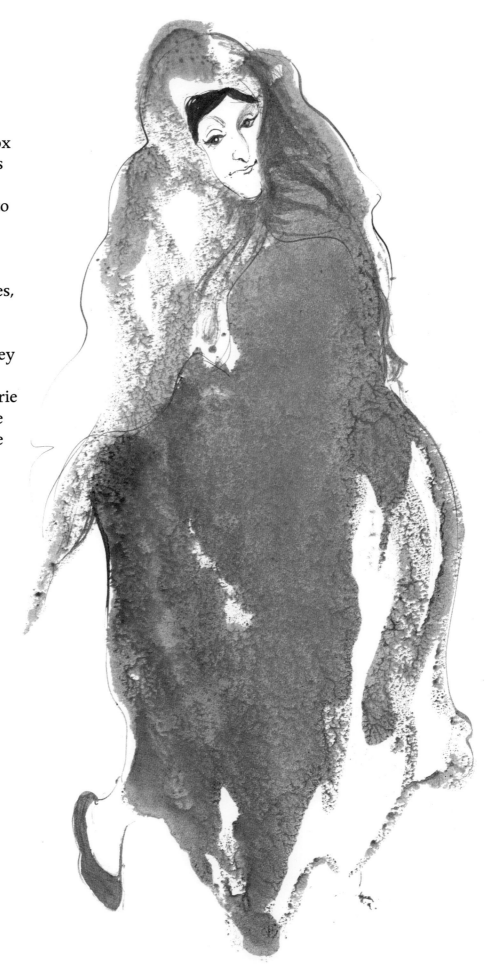

'You like his face? Abdullah come here and be drawn.' A startled Arab stepping through the gate takes one look and bolts. Others are happy to sit. I draw guards, guides, the children who always gather around. Through the gate come endless tourists, most scantily clad. 'Would they,' asks Ali 'go into their churches at home dressed in such a way?' I am told that most of the Arabs who step through are Palestinians, some live in the Old City, more in East Jerusalem. A few have houses on the Mount of Olives, a richer suburb. The villagers come to the Old City to buy and sell. They visit the mosque before returning to Rahmallah, Nablus or Bethlehem. Many Imams, holy men, leaders of prayers in the mosques come through. They will not stop and be drawn either. They wear a red fez with a turban wrapped thirteen times around it. Many are blind and are led by small boys. An Afghan goes through. He wears a large turban, a long white beard and baggy pants. Many Moslem pilgrims come to

Guards & Police at the Chain Gate.

NOTICE & WARNING

ENTRANCE TO THE AREA OF
THE TEMPLE MOUNT IS
FORBIDDEN TO EVERYONE
BY JEWISH LAW. OWING
TO THE SACREDNESS OF
THE PLACE.

THE CHIE RABBINATE OF ISRAEL

خادم الحرم الشريف
AL HARAM AL
SHARIF
GUARD

Sergeant Major.
Mordegia
30 year Service
אורי צריק
יוסף

جمال
عسيله
Jamal
Esayleh.

Arif David Tunge.
who bought my
cigarettes.

Coffee Shop

Jerusalem for it is the third holiest shrine after Mecca and Medina.

A week earlier there had been a strike in the Old City. One early morning I was sitting in the crowded souk. It was business as usual, people pushing and shoving, shouting and cursing, when suddenly there was tangible feeling of tension. Everything vanished in seconds; people, shop owners, all the paraphernalia hanging outside the shops to be replaced by the clang of drawn shutters, and locked doors, and deserted streets save for one bewildered artist. I was told later that any shop that was found open would be stoned. The Egyptian restaurant where I took refuge was one of the unfortunate, his plate-glass window was shattered.

Another day, a Saturday, nothing opened; there was the same eerie feeling of empty echoing streets save for a few puzzled tourists. I thought it was primarily a protest at the signing of the Peace Treaty in Washington. But I was told that a right-wing rabbi had declared he would establish a shrine on the Temple Mount, by force if necessary. 'The Israeli Govern-

ment stops the rabbi like a mother hitting her child, not from the heart' was the consensus of the coffee shops. It was a strange riot with the school children the main protagonists, stones thrown, no serious injuries in the Old City, and at one time all the gates to the Temple Mount closed. The religious Jews I talked to were as indignant as the Arabs, but for another reason. It is against Orthodox Jewish law for a Jew to enter Temple Mount until the Messiah appears. Sir Moses Montifiore, the distinguished British philanthropist who helped the Jews in Jerusalem so much in the mid-nineteenth century, was excommunicated by the Orthodox rabbis for visiting the Mount.

The older Arabs refuse to be drawn into a discussion. They take a more fatalistic view; 'God's will'. The younger are more outspoken. They consider themselves second class citizens, searched and harassed, and even though they admit they are better off materially under

Arab from Bethlehem

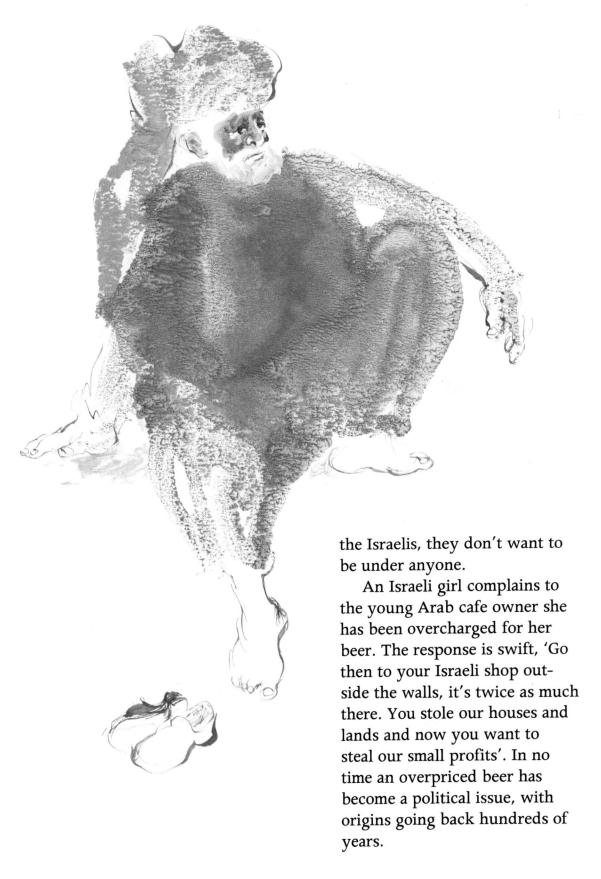

Afghan

the Israelis, they don't want to be under anyone.

An Israeli girl complains to the young Arab cafe owner she has been overcharged for her beer. The response is swift, 'Go then to your Israeli shop outside the walls, it's twice as much there. You stole our houses and lands and now you want to steal our small profits'. In no time an overpriced beer has become a political issue, with origins going back hundreds of years.

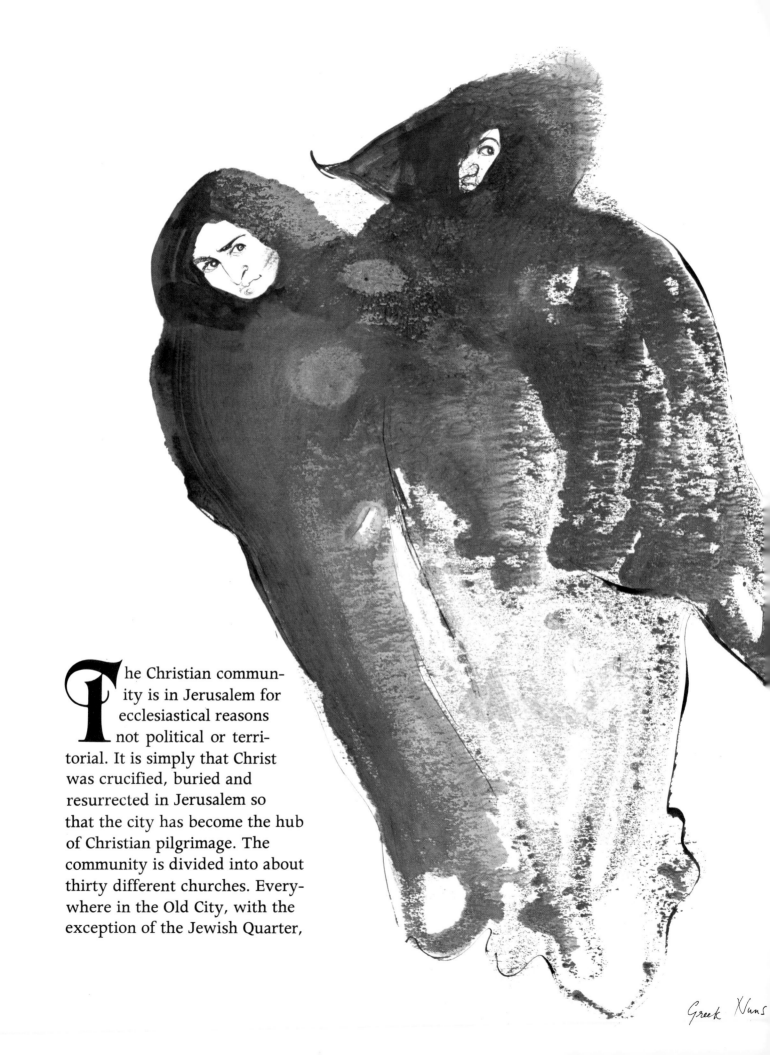

Greek Nuns

The Christian community is in Jerusalem for ecclesiastical reasons not political or territorial. It is simply that Christ was crucified, buried and resurrected in Jerusalem so that the city has become the hub of Christian pilgrimage. The community is divided into about thirty different churches. Everywhere in the Old City, with the exception of the Jewish Quarter,

Hermanns
doing Highland Fling

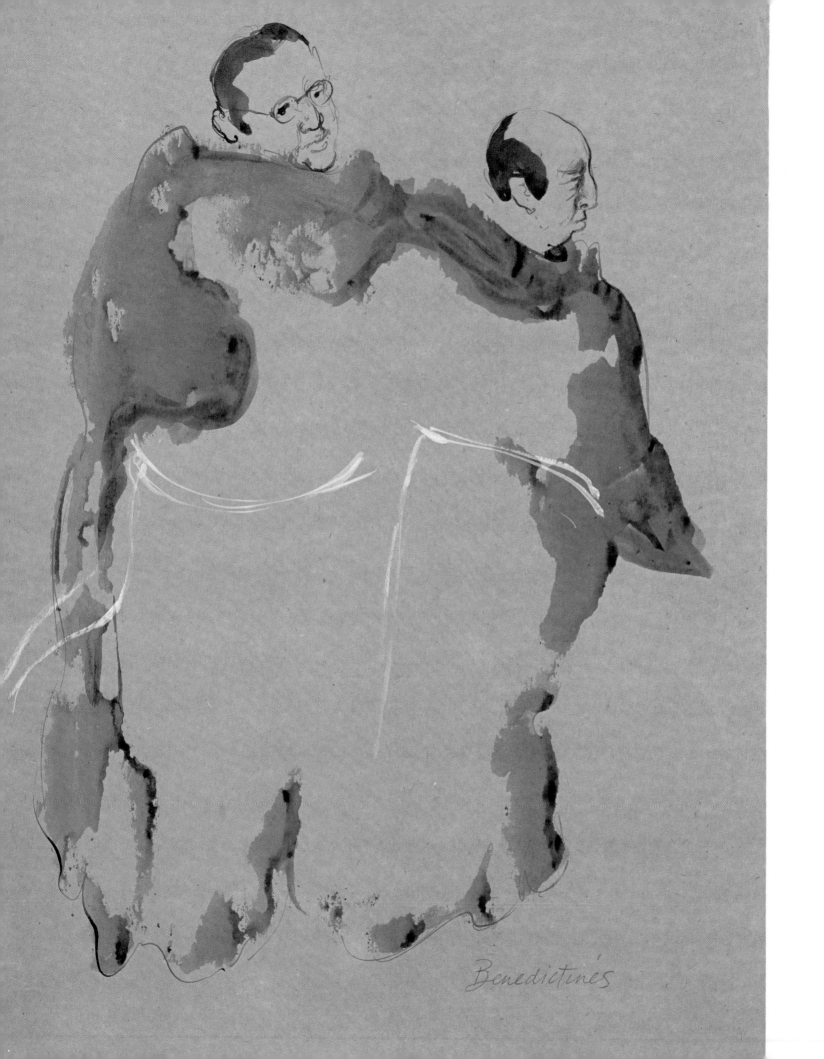

Benedictines

Coptic Monk.

there are churches, monasteries, hospices and missions, and everywhere one sees the black robed, white robed, blue and brown robed figures of the different sects.

The focal point for all Christian pilgrims and for the religious communities is the Church of the Holy Sepulchre. It was built by the decree of the Byzantine Emperor Constantine, whose mother Helena, had identified the site with the tomb of Christ. It has had a chequered history.

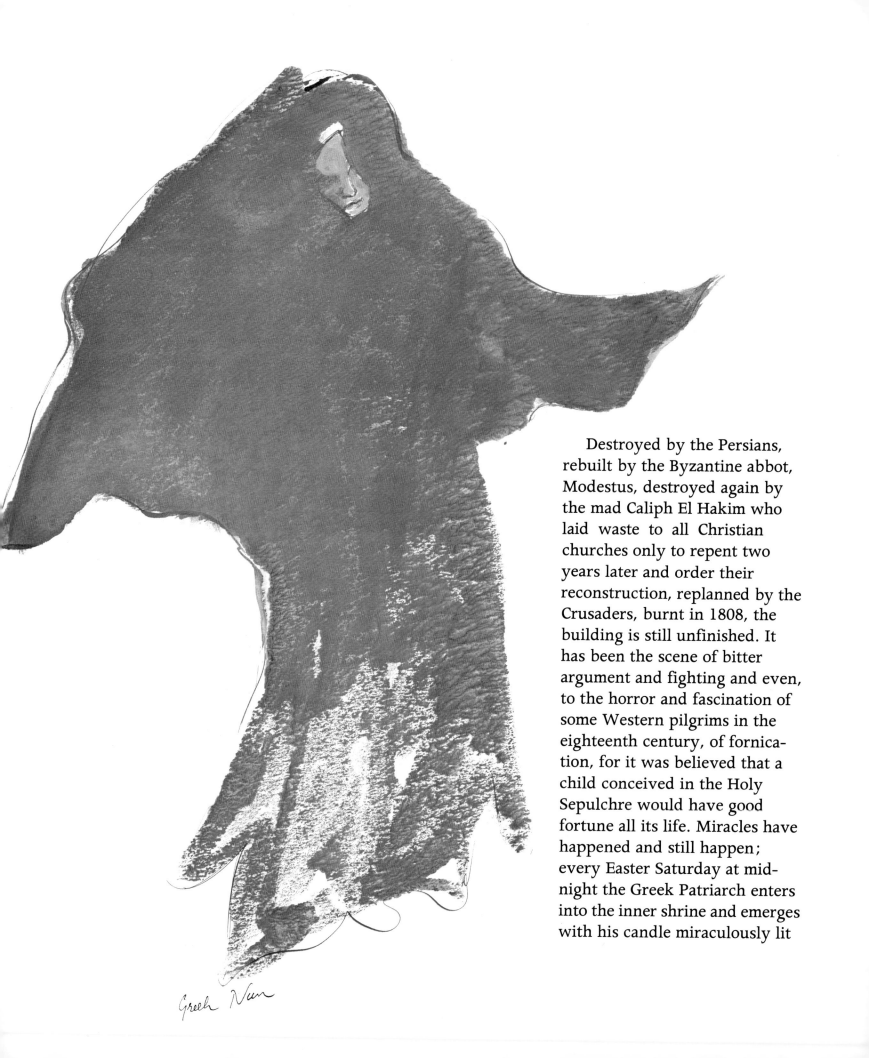

Greek Nun

Destroyed by the Persians, rebuilt by the Byzantine abbot, Modestus, destroyed again by the mad Caliph El Hakim who laid waste to all Christian churches only to repent two years later and order their reconstruction, replanned by the Crusaders, burnt in 1808, the building is still unfinished. It has been the scene of bitter argument and fighting and even, to the horror and fascination of some Western pilgrims in the eighteenth century, of fornication, for it was believed that a child conceived in the Holy Sepulchre would have good fortune all its life. Miracles have happened and still happen; every Easter Saturday at midnight the Greek Patriarch enters into the inner shrine and emerges with his candle miraculously lit

Roman Catholic

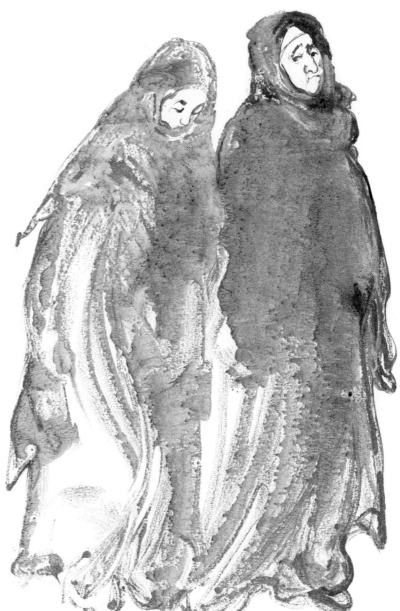

Armenian Nuns

by the Holy Fire. There is a
story that one time the Armenian
Patriarch had to deputize, the
Greek being ill, and to the
satisfaction of the Greeks the
Holy Fire refused to manifest
itself.

There has been much rivalry
among the different Churches
for possession of the different
shrines in the Holy Sepulchre.

In 1852 the Turks passed a decree that the church be partitioned amongst the six communities; the Latins, the Greek Orthodox and the Armenian Orthodox, the major holders, the Copts, Syrian Orthodox and Ethiopians, the minor. Today things are quieter but the rifts are still there. Copt against Ethiopian, Syrian against Armenian, White Russian against Red, Greek Orthodox against the Monophysites. There are internal problems and intrigues too. The election of Patriarchs and the position of the native clergy are but a few of the troubles.

As late as 1973 the Syrians attacked the Armenians whilst they were holding an Easter service in a chapel the Syrians claimed was theirs. By the same decree the Turks made two Moslem families the doorkeepers and key keepers to the church, positions both families hold today. As one Arab explained, it is so that one lot of Christians cannot sneak in and hold more prayers than the other. The biggest space that the Greeks hold in the church is the katholikon, in the middle of which is the Centre of the World. A plaque marks the spot. There is

outside the Sepulchre

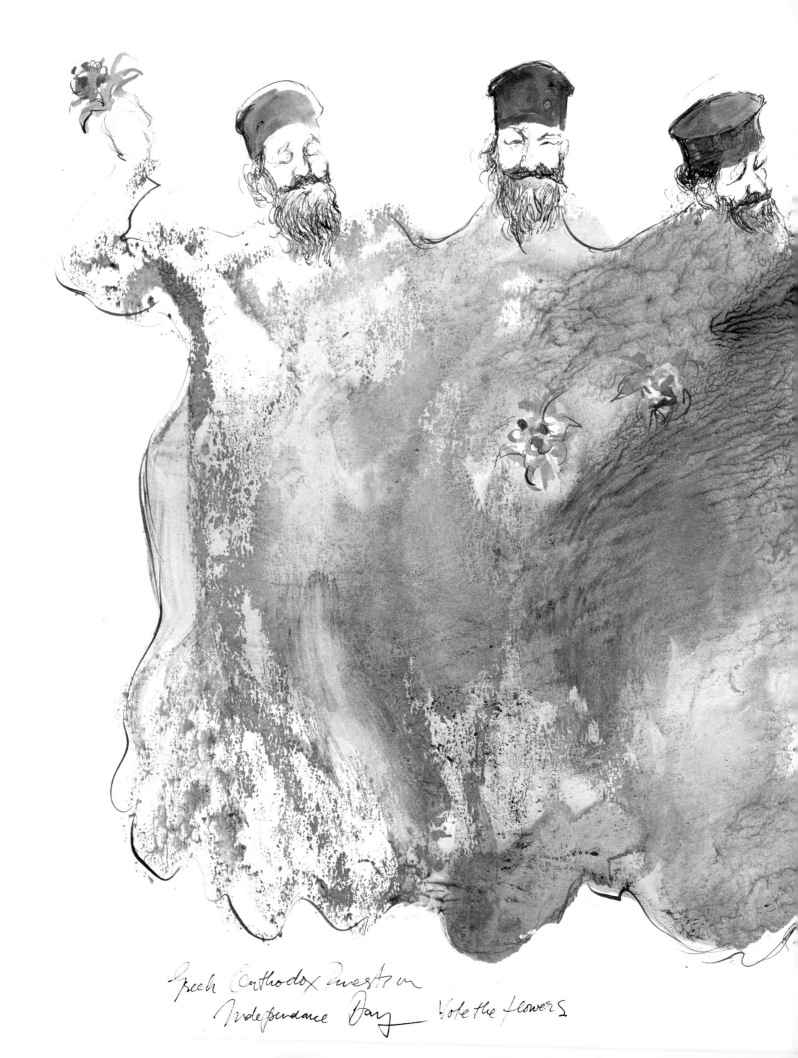

Greek Orthodox Question on
Independence Day — Vote the Flowers

an important celebration here on
25 March, independence day
from 400 years of Turkish rule.
The priests shed their dull robes
for glittering green, yellow and
electric blue. The Consul is there
in a white tie and red sash. It is a
joyful occasion and every priest,
monk and deacon carries a
bouquet of flowers. After the
service there is a procession,
headed by small boys dressed
as evzones and girls as Queen
Amalia, which leads to the Greek
Patriarchate where the Patriarch
sits waiting in the throne room.
His Beatitude, Patriarch Benedictos I, Patriarch since 1958,
is an old man now and he seems
frail as he listens to speeches
about the glory of Greece. Afterwards the procession files past
for the blessings and the kissing
of his hand. I too take my place
in the shuffling queue. Behind
me I hear one old man, excited
that he is showing his respects
on this momentous day in Greek
history, discussing what he will
say to the Patriarch. He whispers
to his friend, 'I'll tell him about
my grandfather whose hand was
shot off at Missolonghi'.

I kiss the small blue hand
and wonder how many times
it has been kissed in the past.

Antonios Galeós.
Ἀντώνιος Χαλέπης
Ἱεροσολυμίτης
1909

works in Rittas
shop.

The Greek Orthodox is the largest religious community and numbers throughout Israel some 38,000, most of whom are Arab. In Jerusalem there are maybe 500 Greeks left and it is sad to wander down Greek Patriarchate Street and see the number of shops with Greek names boarded up. Antonios is one of the few that has returned to Jerusalem. He was born in the Old City but spent most of his life as a teacher in Cyprus. On his retirement he returned to help his old friend Mr Rittas run his shop at the bottom of Casa Nova Street. Many of the Greeks have left since 1967. They could not make a living in Jerusalem, the Israelis made the taxes too high, but, says Antonios, health is the most important thing, not wealth and he is happy to be back. Mr Rittas wanders out from amongst the small chaos of his shop. He sells old sepia postcards; General Allenby entering Jaffa Gate, dashing Arabs galloping in the desert, even some depicting British prisoners under the Turks; old stamps, clothes, old bills that drop out of old books, religious prayers and proverbs; everything is jumbled together with rosaries, crosses, Stars of David, worry beads, Bibles. He is small, old and dusty. He was born in a village near Tripolis in the Peloponnese. Yes, I say, my family is from near Tripolis too.

B. Rutha

P Putras

78 years, arrived in
Jerusalem 1922.

My grandfather was a priest, his name was Economou. There is a small silence. 'Not Papa Economou?! He was my teacher!! In Nea Hori!' He runs to embrace me. He makes a long speech on the glorious sons of the Peloponnese; how if it were not for Kolokotronis there would be no democracy in Greece, in Europe or the world for that matter. At the same time he shovels crucifixes and camels and postcards into my arms. Maybe miracles do happen in Jerusalem; to travel half way round the world to find someone who knew my grandfather who died in a tiny village in the middle of the Peloponnese sixty-five years ago!

I had been given an introduction to Archbishop Vassilios, one of the hierarchy of the Patriarchate and a member of the Brotherhood of the Tomb, the hundred members of which safeguard the Greek shrines. Their emblem is displayed on the bridge that links the Patriarchate with the Monastery of St Nicholas. The bridge was built so that the Patriarch did not have to descend to street level when he wished to visit the monastery. It is here that

the Archbishop has his office.
A small room lined with books
and stuffed, hardback chairs. It
has a pleasant brown glow in
contrast to the blinding white
outside.

The Archbishop is having a
spot of trouble. A girl has
arrived to ask for money she
claims her uncle has sent her
from Athens. It seems the
Patriarchate frequently acts as
bank for the Greeks staying
temporarily in Jerusalem. The
Archbishop has not heard from
the uncle; the girl cannot remember where he lives or what
work he does but she knows
his name. The Archbishop de-
murs; it is difficult to give
money without receiving it first.
How long has the girl been in
Jerusalem? A year and this is
the first time she has come to
the Patriarchate! He is upset
but agrees, as she is in trouble,
to give her half of what the
uncle has supposedly sent. The
girl inexplicably refuses and
runs out to join the boy she
came with.

Vassilios is perplexed by
her behaviour. Youth no longer
has respect for the Church. He
offers coffee and cognac,
traditional standbys of Greek

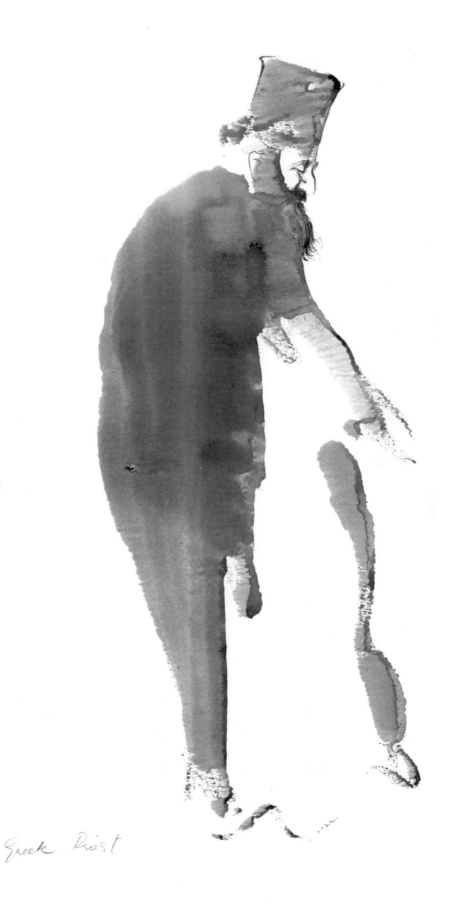

Greek Priest

H.A.Θ.M. O. ΠΑΤΡΙΑΧΗΣ ΙΕΡΟΣΟΛΥΜΩΝ
ΒΕΝΕΔΙΚΤΟΣ. A'

Patriarcha of Jerusalem
Benedictos 1st.

hospitality. He is from Argos and has been in Jerusalem thirty years. He asked if I would like to attend the Patriarch's name day on Tuesday. It might be possible to draw his Beatitude if I arrive early enough.

The Greek Orthodox is the oldest Church in Jerusalem (a claim that all the other Orthodox Churches make), and one of the richest with many schools, missions and monasteries. The first Greeks to come to the city were with Alexander the Great. The next influx were the Byzantines. The schism with the other Orthodox Churches occurred in 451 at the Council of Chalcedon. The Greeks stuck to the doctrine of the Trinity, the others claimed that Christ had a composite nature, hence they became known as the Mono-physites. Vassilios hopes that the Eastern Churches will get together again but, he reflects sadly, they still don't see our point of view. At the same Council Jerusalem became a see and the Bishop of Jerusalem a Patriarch. Patriarch Benedictos is the thirty-ninth in succession.

Early on Tuesday I am again at the Patriarchate. This time I sit in a room surrounded by

ὁ Μητροπολίτης Κεισαρείας
Θεόφιλος.

⊤ = Τάφος = Tomb
or
Τάφου Φύλακες Tomb's Guardians.

Θεοδόσιος
Αρχιεπίσκοπος
Ιερουσαλήμ 22-3-79

Archbishop Vassilios
Greek Orthodox

Russian Nuns

giggling school girls in blue
uniforms and gentle-faced nuns.
They are the pupils of the
Bethany Russian Orthodox
School and are going to sing in
Russian for the Patriarch. They
are all Arab except one small
Greek girl. The nuns are White
Russians and their Church is
administered from New York,
the Russian Church in Exile.
Looking at their faces one could
believe the tradition of the
aristocratic families in Russia

putting their younger daughters
in the Church. It is said that a
niece of Czar Nicholas still lives
in a Russian convent in
Jerusalem and at St Alexander's
Church prayers are said each
Thursday for the soul of Czar
Alexander III. There are two
Russian Orthodox Missions in
Jerusalem, the one White, the
other Red, both of them
administered from Moscow.

Their large compound is outside the Old City, a short distance from New Gate.

On my way to the throne room I pass Vladimir, the administrator of the compound. His daughter, who is dressed in peasant costume, will present flowers to the Patriarch.

He prefers to sit apart from the White Russians. An Israeli friend told me of her encounter with the Red Russians. She had to interview them and for some time afterwards received 'phone calls from a mysterious man anxious to meet her. She finally agreed to a rendezvous and it transpired her caller worked for the Israeli secret police. He wanted to know full details of the Russian interpreter at the compound. My friend could not give much information as to her he was just the interpreter for the answers to the questions she asked the Archbishop. A few days later she read that the interpreter had been expelled by the Israeli Government. He was a senior member of the KGB.

The Patriarch seems smaller today and more weighed down with medallions and sashes. I kiss his hand and request

Russian Monk.

permission to draw him. Before
he can reply his assistant, tall
and crow-like, says no, it's impossible, do I not realize what
day it is, they will all be coming
from the Holy Sepulchre now.
He is swept aside by his Beatitude who asks me where I am
from, what I am doing, please
be seated and start drawing.
My task is hampered by the
assistant. He chivvies me along,
peers over my shoulder, sneers
and says, 'It's only lines'. I am
not sure what else he expected.
I finish a sketchy outline before
the doors open and a wave of
black robes and stovepipes
sweep in. 'Did you draw him?'
whispers Vassilios. 'Sort of' I
nod and retire to the rear of
the room.

The room is jammed, everyone pushing to kiss the Patriarch's hand, to wish him
'Many years' and to give him
flowers or gifts. Deacons elbow
their way through the throng
with trays loaded with coffee
and cognac. Toasts are drunk,
speeches made. Israel is never
mentioned, it would appear that
the country is still Palestine
as far as the Greek Orthodox
are concerned. The Bethany
Choir sings an off-key anthem,

Greek Orthodox Priest

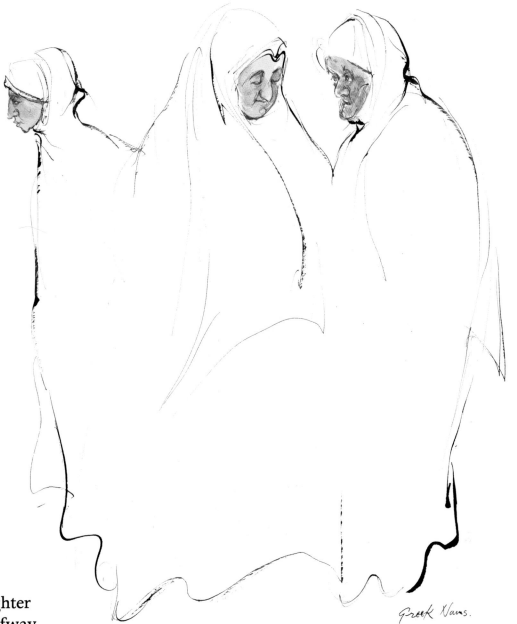

Greek Nuns.

the Administrator's daughter
presents the flowers. Halfway
through the proceedings the
voice of a muezzin from the
nearby mosque drowns the
speeches. The whole affair
has an unreal air as though one
has been transported back in
time.

Traditionally the Churches
are supported to a sizable degree
by the pilgrims. The Greek
Orthodox attract large numbers.
The Old City during Holy Week

David Street

is transformed into a Greek village. The buses unload at Jaffa Gate as usual. Gone are the tourists and their matching hats to be replaced by rotund Greek village priests waving umbrellas and endeavouring, mostly unsuccessfully, to keep their errant flocks in line. I saw more traditional Greek costumes during one day in Jerusalem than I have seen in all my wanderings through Greece. These people, old men, widows and nuns, have saved for a lifetime in their remote villages to make a pilgrimage to the Holy City. The ultimate reward for their journey will be a large, elaborately decorated scroll that proclaims them *hadjis*, pilgrims, who have visited all the Greek shrines in the Holy Land of Palestine.

All the shopkeepers suddenly speak Greek and the haggling and screaming is pitched decibels higher for each Greek Pilgrim is convinced that the Arab shop-owners are out to strip them of their every drachma. I passed one woman who had bought a bread roll from a street vendor. She clutched both roll and money and demanded that she be given her change before she parted with her ten lira note.

'Gin and tonic? Or maybe a campari soda?'
The room is airy and modern with a stereo record player and tapedeck, a large television set and many display cupboards full of intricate and beautiful glassware.

'That is my hobby, collecting antique glass. I go anywhere in the world to see or buy it.'

The speaker is Archbishop Shahe Ajamian of the Armenian Orthodox Church, prominent in the World Council of Churches. With us is Yehudi Menuhin, his wife and son. He is in Jerusalem to do a series of concerts with his son, a pianist. He says he cannot exactly be classified as an inhabitant of the Old City but he does have connections. His father and

Archbishop SHAHÉ AJAMIAN

Armenian Prelates

grandfather lived here for some time. He himself came for the first time in 1950. Not a particularly happy visit for the Irgun were upset with him for giving a concert in Germany and everywhere he went he was accompanied by a bodyguard. Since then he has returned innumerable times and a few days ago he had stood two hours in the rain at the Wailing Wall to play a tribute to the signing of the Peace Treaty.

We had met amongst angels, miniature dragons, harpies, elaborate birds, kings, man-swallowing whales and flowers. Our guide was an austere, stern monk with a great love and reverence for his several thousand charges, the illuminated manuscripts of the Armenian convent. The ones he shows us are truly remarkable; the colours golds, pinks, ochres, dusty blues and the text so exact that it appears typeset, only there were no printing presses in the tenth and eleventh centuries. One wonders about those long ago artists, the patience and craftsmanship needed to produce such beautiful things. In some of the manuscripts there is mention of them and the hardships they had to endure while working. One artist in particular writes that he could never complete his work in one place as he was constantly pursued by Mongols.

Armenians have been a presence in Jerusalem since early times. One Armenian king, Tigranes II, even included Palestine and Jerusalem in his empire for a brief while. After the schism with the Greeks at Chalcedon the Armenian Church was recognized as the head of the other Monophysite Churches, the Coptic, Ethiopian and Jacobian. The first Patriarch was installed in Caliph Omar's time and the monastery of St James, above which I was now sitting, was built towards the end of the seventeenth century to house not only the monks but also the many pilgrims. A British traveller in the mid-nineteenth century said it was the only place in Jerusalem that had an air of cleanliness and wealth about it.

House of Annas.
Armenian Convent of Nuns
Church of Archangels

The Armenian Quarter or Compound is like a small city within a city. It was transformed at the turn of the century after the Armenian massacres in Turkey caused destitute refugees to start flooding into Jerusalem, a sorry contrast to the wealthy pilgrims of previous centuries. They were allowed to stay, gratis, in the compound provided they observed the rules of the monasteries, one of which still survives. At 9 p.m. every night the gates to the compound close. There are about three thousand Armenians in Jerusalem but many, like the Greeks, have left to make more money overseas. An Armenian shirtmaker told me that his son is now a vice president of Holiday Inns in America. 'He makes $70,000 a year but I wonder is he really happy?' He has not seen his son since he left.

In the compound are shops,
a clinic, the first printing press
to be established in Jerusalem,
a museum, an Armenian school
with 300 pupils, a public library,
a seminary and the monastery
itself with its twenty-five monks.
I am introduced to Father Vartabed Parilonysian, Father Good
Morning. He is a magnificent
old man, eighty-four years old,
over six feet tall, with an open
face, long Santa Claus beard
and very blue eyes. He was
born in Moussada, Turkey, but
managed to escape to Athens.
He has been a monk for over
fifty years and came to Jerusalem because 'God sent me'.

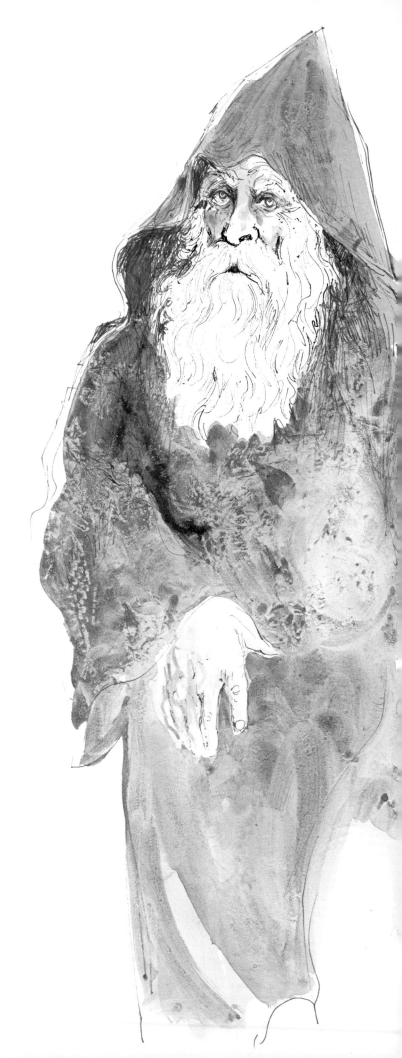

Ռեֆ...

Father. Mashtodz Vartabed.
Parilouyshian.
·family name means good Morning.

...

Khatchig Souyoutian.

Karekian. Checkmian.
Armenian. Tailor.

I tell him he has a beautiful face, so he smiles and says it is beautiful because he is with Christ. My interpreter is a young deacon, also from Turkey, a graduate of the seminary, the qualification for which he tells me is a good voice. He takes me to his cell to listen to Armenian music. Other monks and deacons wander in.

At first sight, particularly when seen in the dark alleys of the Old City, there is something sinister about the pointed hoods of the monks, one cannot but help draw analogies with the Ku Klux Klan and secret societies. But these monks are anything but sinister. They laugh and joke, particularly about my drawings: 'Why you've made him look Chinese.' I ask one to sign his name on his portrait. He has told me he can speak English, Armenian and Turkish. Would he sign in all three languages. The first two certainly, Turkish never: 'I wish to forget that country.' Most people know little of the massacres, indeed to this day the Turks refuse to admit they have ever taken

place. There are photographs
in the school of mounds of
corpses, hangings, executions;
1,500,000 people 'disappeared'
at that time, half the population
of Armenia. The Archbishop is
worried about another group
of Armenians. There are 200,000
of them in Iran and he is afraid
of what will happen to them.
Already the Jews are starting to
be persecuted.

Within the compound is the
Convent of the Olive Tree, the
tree to which Christ was supposedly tied. One nun lives
there. Educated in a Greek convent in Constantinople she
speaks fluent Greek besides
Armenian. She also speaks
Turkish, although like the
monks she wishes to forget
that country. She is happy,
she has her garden, her small
house and her church, why
think of terrible things.

Sister Deree Garabekian.

Church of Arch Angels.
House of High Priest Annas

On the way back I am shown
the Cathedral of St James the
Greater, the Apostle who was
beheaded by Herod Agrippa I,
and St James the Less, cousin
of Jesus and the first Christian
Bishop of Jerusalem. He is buried
under the altar. It is dim inside,
richly carpeted, ornate with
carved thrones, pearly lecterns
and the smell of incense. On
the floor a woman is repairing

Father Justine

Fr. Justin Belitz

From America. Omaha
Nebraska

Franciscan Friar

Father Basilio Tealatinian
been in Jerusalem since 39 years
Back

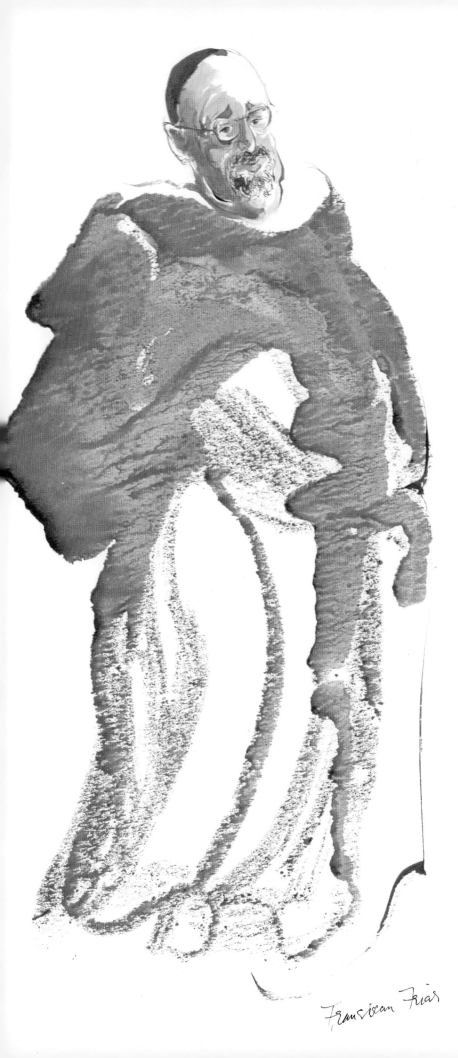

Franciscan Friar

the huge embroidered cloth that hangs behind the altar. Each month it is changed, each month she searches for new damage in the old cloth. Outside the cathedral are wooden 'clappers'. The Turks forbade the Christians to ring bells so the clappers were used as a substitute. By the same token no Christian or Jewish shrine or building could be higher than the Dome of the Rock and beside most churches and synagogues in the Old City there is a mosque. The muezzins would tolerate no competition.

One of the cheapest places to eat in the Old City is the Casa Nova Hospice run by the Franciscans. One sits in a long room at a long table with benign angels and Virgin Marys peering from the walls. The wine is plentiful, the food Italian Arab, the company varied; a sprinkling of brown robed monks, nuns, Italian and German pilgrims, Japanese tourists and the regulars. Mr Mansour, a Roman Catholic, has spent much of his life working for the Red Cross and for refugees in Jerusalem, and now in his old age, runs a small antique shop. His friend, elegant in suit, tie and waistcoat, is the teacher of English at the Greek Orthodox school. His wife is brown and sparrow-like and for an Arab woman very talkative. She discourses on every subject nonstop, the Palestinian question, American politics, the price of bread, all the time gesticulating, her mouth full, only stopping occasionally to drain her wine glass.

Every now and again one is interrupted by a burst of song from some of the jollier friars at the end of the table. The wine is excellent, very strong and grown by the Franciscans at one of their monasteries outside Jerusalem.

Every denomination has its hospice. An English traveller in the nineteenth century remarked that the Casa Nova was passable, the Armenian the cleanest and the Greek the worst, the beds being full of bedbugs. Another pilgrim of the sixteenth century declared he preferred to stay with the Franciscans as the Abbot himself washed the feet of the dusty travellers. Now the line between pilgrim and tourist is thin and most choose to stay at one of the hotels outside the city walls.

The Knight's Palace Hotel, just up the road from the Casa Nova, used to be a hospice too. It has the same plaster saints on the walls but here they have a forlorn, neglected air. Aboud is the barman and serves breakfast in the echoing refectory. He is Catholic and has two problems, his teeth which are new and uncontrollable and his wife who is, he claims giggling, a dragon and beats him all the time. He lives in the Moslem Quarter near the Damascus Gate.

I was introduced to St Saviour's Monastery, the Franciscan headquarters of Jerusalem and the Middle East, by Friar Justin. The Franciscans are much the biggest Order amongst the Roman Catholics. After the Crusaders and Frankish Kings were finally thrown out by the Saracens,

Roman Catholic Bishops

Kawass for
Greek Orthodox Church
on Independence Day.

Reshed Aly Sish Lawi
Kawass.

the Franciscans moved in to establish a Latin presence again in the Holy Land. They were granted a Patriarchate in the twelfth century and became the official guardians of the Roman Catholic shrines. There are about 20,000 Catholics in Israel, most of them Arab.

Friar Justin had been introduced to me by Abraham, one of the Kawasses of the monastery. The Kawasses are the general factotums of the different Christian Churches. They run errands, act as guides, gatekeepers, coffee servers but most important they head the processions. One is always notified of the approach of a procession by the steady thump of their staffs on the flagstones. They wear red tarbouches, carry riding whips to beat the donkeys out of the way, but their uniforms vary.

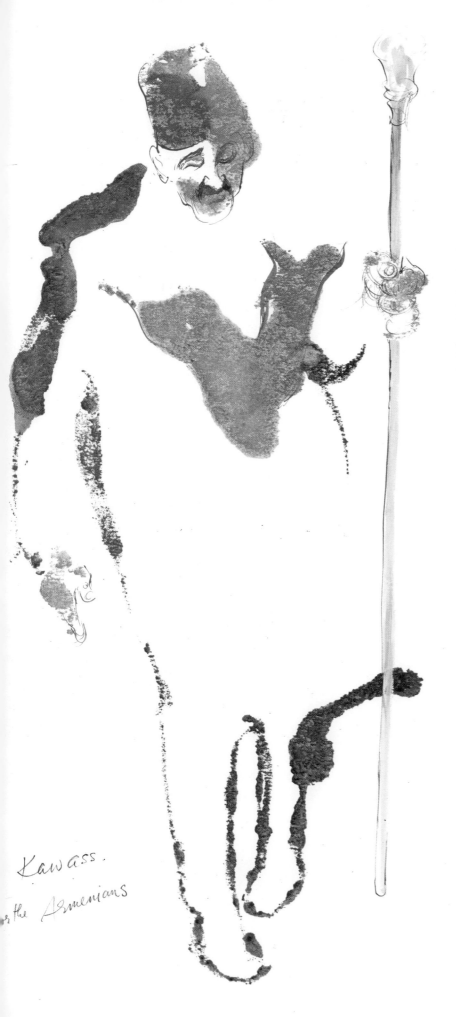

Kawass.
the Armenians

Abraham wears a green suit, his Armenian counterpart blue with a red collar but the most resplendent uniform I saw was that of the Greek Kawass. For the Patriarch's birthday party he wore a magnificent bright blue embroidered waistcoat, a white shirt with wide sleeves and the baggy pants favoured by the Cretans. The wide cut with the big bag behind is to save Christ from hitting the ground, for the Cretans believe that one of them will give birth to the new Messiah.

Friar Justin is an American who is teaching for a while in Jerusalem. His students are deacons who will be ordained in a few months and his most popular class is the one on the Silva method of mind control. He feels strongly that a lot of the doctrine and teaching is far too staid and that the Church should get more 'with it'. He takes me to the common room where a number of deacons are sprawled watching the first colour television I have seen in Jerusalem. None of the Israeli

Brother. Mario.
from Malta.
Camilleri Jr.

Brother Jack Taram.
from Nazareth.

programmes is in colour yet but it is easy to pick up Jordanian programmes. Most people in Jerusalem prefer to watch Jordanian television
anyway because many of the programmes are from the BBC;
Upstairs, *Downstairs* was a firm favourite, followed by *The Brothers*. It
seems strange that the inhabitants of Jerusalem should find so much
pleasure in such quintessentially English programmes.

It is Friar Justin's birthday and I am invited to a party that the deacons
have arranged as a surprise at the Swedish Mission outside the Old City.
The deacons have all changed into jeans and are indistinguishable from
the other young people in the streets. One, from Malta, explains that they
always wear 'mufti' in West Jerusalem because if they wear their robes
they are mocked and given a hard time. He has been in Jerusalem a couple
of years but is looking forward to his return to Malta. His family will
come to Jerusalem for his ordination, the first time they have left the
island.

Friar Justin is overcome by his 'surprise'. The other guests are all pupils from his class on mind control. There are several nuns, mostly from Malta, two missionaries, some Swedish, the deacons and a dour German writer. My Maltese friend says that he has enjoyed the classes very much, they have given him much to think about, but at times he has found it difficult to project himself into a tea kettle. One of the requirements is apparently to become part of an inanimate object. There is much bantering and laughter. Wine flows freely, there is masses of food and a large birthday cake; the nuns present Friar Justin with a beautiful cross and chain. It is for his mother as under Franciscan vows he cannot accept any gifts. One of the deacons arranges the group for a photograph. 'Come on Sister, cuddle closer to Father Justin!' We pose but then amid much hilarity he realizes he has forgotten to bring a flashbulb.

The whole occasion seemed far removed from my preconceived ideas of monkish cells and vows of silence, self-flagellation and tonsured heads.

There are of course many other religious orders in Jerusalem: Benedictines, Dominicans, Carmelites, the White Fathers, to name a few; in all sixteen male orders and twenty-six female.

The White Fathers are responsible for the Church of St Anne, close to St Stephen's Gate. Built by the Crusaders it was made into a Moslem seminary by the Saracens. After the Crimean War the Turks gave the church and the adjacent site of the Pool of Bethesda to the French government as a small 'thank you' for their help in the war. Although it is still the property of the French government, it is served by the White Fathers. They are an order of missionaries who started in North Africa. 'But', says Brother Bill, 'they didn't do too well. A lot were murdered so they decided to go deeper into Africa. These were mostly killed as well but the few that survived started missions in Uganda, Zaire, Tanzania, Malawi and Zanzibar.'

Brother Bill (Wim)
from Holland.

White Father

Brother Bill has been ten years in Jerusalem and looks after the small gift shop. He is pleased because he has sold two Bibles today. He is from Holland, his real name is Wim but everyone calls him Bill. He finds it amusing that I should wish to draw him but enters into the spirit of it and when I have finished runs out to catch another White Father. He reappears with Father Magnin from France. The White Fathers wear a robe similar to the Bedouin jellaba. It is white to reflect the sun and has a tasselled hood. Father Magnin tells me there are 3,000 members of the order, forty-seven of whom are permanently based in Jerusalem. The mission here is used as a retreat. I would imagine it is most welcome after the jungle and turmoil of countries like Uganda and Tanzania.

My last image of Brother Bill is of him holding a large rock in his hand trying to open the solid oak door to the mission. It has stuck and he is bashing it hard with his rock aided by several laughing Arab children.

There are several other Catholic Churches in Jerusalem. There are the Melkite or Greek Catholic whose Archbishop has recently been expelled for smuggling weapons for the Palestinians into Israel under his robes. There are Armenian Catholics, and Syrian Catholics, Chaldeans and Maronites, most of them breakaways from the Orthodox Churches, who follow the Byzantine as opposed to the Latin rites.

Father Pierre Magnin
White Father

P. Magnin   LoRRAINE.

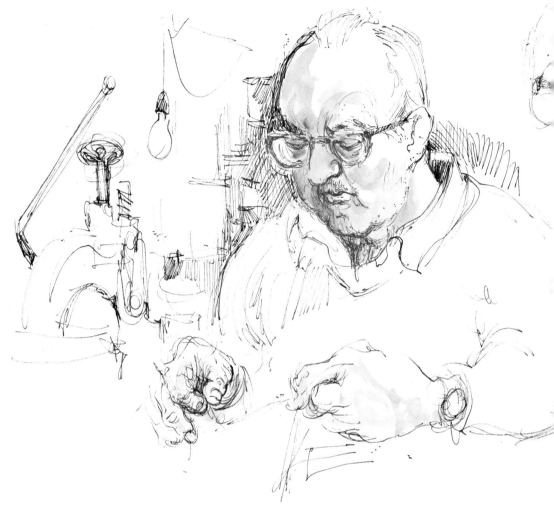

Armenian
Book Binder

I was going to school for the first time
& there were some carriages drawn by horses.
one of the wheels from the carriages flew
off & struck me. — & thats how I lost my
leg. —   They, that is my parents, wanted
me to be a tailor — some job that, what they
though an invalid like me could do. — Any
way, this didnt suit me So I became a book
binder.

Jean Persekian

PERSEKIAN'S
ARTISTIC BINDERY
NEW-GATE
JERUSALEM

RESIDENCE
Tel. 856503

WORK
Tel. 282811

ALBUMS
CARTONNAGE
BOOK-BINDING
CUTLERY BOXES
JEWELLERY BOXES

PERSEKIAN
BOOKBINDER · BOXMAKER
JERUSALEM ☎ 2811
JORDAN

Farag Nazrala
Assistant, chief director, father of six children

Mr Persekian is an Armenian Catholic. He is a bookbinder and boxmaker in the Christian Quarter. His father was a baker with the Turkish army and came to Jerusalem with them because no one else could equal his bread. Mr Persekian was born here and at an early age was run over by a cart on his way to school. As there was no penicillin he contracted gangrene and his leg was amputated. But he says, as he hops around his shop, he has been so long with one leg that he cannot remember what it is like to have two. He became a bookbinder because his parents regarded him as an invalid and incapable of following his father into the bakery. The choice was tailoring or bookbinding. He chose the latter. Now he and his Arab assistant have more work than they can manage, particularly the presentation boxes. While I was there he completed one order for the Bezalel Art School in West Jerusalem and started on another for the Greek Orthodox Patriarchate. His customers come from everywhere.

There is a shortage of space in the Holy Sepulchre. On a Sunday it seems ready to burst its walls with the congregations, the chanting, the liturgies, the priests and deacons of the different sects. The Greeks, Latins and Armenians have the largest and best lit spaces, the Copts occupy a small area behind the shrine and the Syrians a tiny, dim chapel which once belonged to the Armenians.

Of the Ethiopians there is no sign. They occupy the roof of the Holy Sepulchre and hold their services in the chapels of the Four Living Things and St Michael and All Saints. There are no pews in the chapels, the monks lean on their prayer sticks and the service is conducted in the ancient language of Ge'ez.

To reach the monastery one goes through the crowded, noisy souk past the butchers and sweet sellers, up some steps, through a small gate into a different world. A tranquil open courtyard in the centre of which is the cupola of the Chapel of St Helena; it is fringed by trees, bird song and curious mud structures suggestive of

Ethiopian Monastery of Deir el Sultan

አባ፡ ገብረ፡ መድኅን፡

Abar gebra medin

an African village. These are the cells of the monks and repairs cannot be carried out because of a dispute that has been simmering between the Copts and Ethiopians for nearly 150 years.

It is a long story. One of the first Ethiopians to visit Jerusalem was the Queen of Sheba. She apparently foresaw the coming of Christ and declared that there should always be an Ethiopian presence in Jerusalem. Later, the Empress Helena of the Byzantines remembered and set aside places for Ethiopian chapels. At first there were plenty of pilgrims and donations, and the Ethiopians had many monasteries, churches and shrines in the Holy Sepulchre. Then, due to political upheavals in Ethiopia, they were unable to pay the Turkish taxes and bribes, so they lost everything save the monastery on the roof and two chapels.

Tragedy struck in the form of the plague and all the monks died. Before replacements from Ethiopia could be sent the Copts moved in and took the two chapels and the passageway to the Holy Sepulchre, a shortcut from their monastery of St Anthony's to the church. The

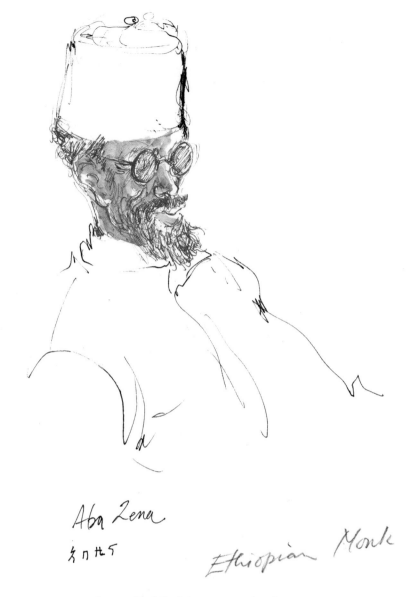

Aba Zena
አባ ዘና
Ethiopian Monk

Turks upheld this action and so the Ethiopians lost access to the Holy Sepulchre and their chapels until 1970.

On Easter eve while the Copts were praying in the Holy Sepulchre the Ethiopians changed the locks to the doors of the chapels without interference from the many Israeli police in the courtyard. The Copts finished their service and to their surprise and rage found they could no longer use their short cut or the chapels. The police stopped them breaking the doors down so they took the matter straight to the Israeli courts. The High Court upheld the Coptic rights but the Israeli government intervened and froze the situation until it could be amicably settled. And that is how it stands today. The Ethiopians are not allowed to make repairs until the dispute is resolved so they continue to live in their tumbledown, leaking mud cells.

Not surprisingly they have the most positive view towards Israel of any of the various Churches I met. Several monks are learning Hebrew taught by a Danish nun who joined the Ethiopian Church fifteen years ago. Previously she had been a Roman Catholic but after a visit to the Holy Land felt that the Ethiopians were the simplest, least regimented order and the truest to the original meaning of Christianity: 'There is too much bureaucracy in the Church nowadays.'

She is a remarkable woman. Since September 1977, the Ethiopians had been without an Archbishop, though one arrived soon after our visit. Emahoy Krestos Samra is helping to look after Ethiopian affairs from her tiny office at the Archbishop's house. She also finds time to teach English, history, Hebrew, French, German and Arabic within the community. Twice a week she gives lessons in Ethiopian ikon painting. One of her ikons hangs in the office, a powerful, primitive head of Christ. As if this is not enough she is writing, in Hebrew, a thesis on the history of the Ethiopians for the Hebrew University. She will be glad to finish this project as it will give her more time to paint ikons. Twice during my visit we were interrupted by groups of Israelis wishing to see slides and reproductions of the different styles of Ethiopian iconography.

There are forty-four Ethiopian monks and nuns in Israel, eighteen in the monastery on the roof. The monks sit around their courtyard, some learning Hebrew verbs (I am told there are many similarities between Hebrew and Amharic, modern Ge'ez), some gazing into space and one always on duty at the door to the chapels. They take great delight in

Ethiopian Nun. Emohoy Christo Samra. and one of her icons

Coptic Orthodox
Monastery.
Monastery of the Sultan.

being drawn, giggling through their hands when shown the finished product. One is struck by their gentleness and serenity as well as by the poverty in which they live.

The same feeling of serenity pervades the monastery of their neighbours and rivals, the Copts. One steps through the door from the Ethiopians, up some steps and one is immediately outside the Monastery of St Athony. An old Arab, Achmed, is permanently positioned here and for a small consideration he will show one the Ninth Station of the Cross, the Church of St Helena and the monastery. It is built around a courtyard, peaceful and glowing from the orange ochre paint of its walls.

I climbed zigzagging iron staircases past schoolrooms and at the second level I was met by a large happy figure in the black robes and bonnet of the Coptic monk. This was Archbishop Vassilios, the Coptic Orthodox Archbishop of Jerusalem and the Near East. On hearing that I wished to draw him he went to change his robes ('These are much too dusty') and his hat. I talk to the headmistress of the Coptic school who is

ΠΙΔΙΠΠΔΤΙΔΡΧΗC ΠΡΕΜΠΧΗΜΙ
+
ΠΟΡΘΟΔΟΖΟC

اسم الكنيسة هيلانة الملكة الاروذكسية

Written by
the hand of Nasef.
Shukri. Tadros
from Egypt.
(Student Priest.)

ΤΗC NOΡΗΟΔΖΟC
+
QUEEN HELEN CHURCH
COPTIC ORTHODOX.

Entrance
Coptic Monastery.

الراهب عبدالله
الانبا بولس

Father Abden
Melek.

Aymat
Galiel.
"Guard"

احمد خليل

sitting behind an antique type-writer in the Archbishop's office. She acts as his secretary besides being headmistress to nine hundred pupils. The Coptic community is large, three thousand in Jerusalem alone. The Archbishop returns. Besides Coptic, Arabic and English he speaks Greek because he studied religious history at the University of Thessaloniki for several years. He tells me a little of Coptic history. The Copts came to Jerusalem under the auspices of St Athanasios in the fourth century and with the consecration of the Holy Sepulchre established a monastery.

In the past they had always been a wealthy community, three to four thousand pilgrims a year, but since the Six Day War there have been no pilgrimages and no contributions.

At the Entrance to the
Coptic Orthodox Monastery.
My young friend
Spent the morning watching me
work. — Wonderful past-time
fetching me tea — water &
interpreting — when needed.

Nassef Shukri Tadros.
from Egypt.

AL giza

قبطي شكري تادرس

Egypt   الجيزة

Walking around the monastery one can see vestiges of former wealth in the numbers of large rooms with fading wall paint and deteriorating furniture. He himself goes to Egypt quite frequently by way of the Gaza Strip and Sinai and now with the opening of the borders he hopes the pilgrimages will resume. He makes no mention of the quarrel with the Ethiopians but it seems a shame that the two poorest Churches are at loggerheads.

Father Nabir
Coptic Monk

القس ميناء الانطوني

Nabir. ANTY. NE

✝ BACIΛΕΙΟC

رتبة الاساقفة
الكندر الانبا باسيليوس
ميتروبوليت كرسي الاسكندرية والشرق الادنى
للاقباط الارثوذكس

His Grace Vassilios.
The Coptic Orthodox
Archbishop of Jerusalem & N. East

Syrian Father Elias
from Tor Abdin - Turkey
arrived 2 years ago.

... And his writings

ܚܕܐ ܘܡܢܗܘܢ
ܢܩܐܡ ܐܝܟܐ. ܕܗܝ ܠܟܐ
ܟܠ ܠܚܡܝܐ ܡܢ ܡܢܗ. ܠܐܚܡ
ܝܕܥ ܗܘܐ ܘܠܐܝܢܫ ܝܕܥ
ܡܝܢ ܠܠܐ. ܘܗܝ ܘܝܫ ܟܠܐ
ܐܘܗܡܝܫ ܝܠܠܐ ..

Syrian Orthodox Jacobite Church

'The Syrians were the first Christians.' Each Church has made a similar claim but Father Yacoub expounds his theory. At the time of Christ Greek was the official language but the people spoke Aramaic and the first Bibles were written in Aramaic. The Arameans changed their name to Syrian at the time of Christ and Aramaic became Syriac.

Whatever the theories the Syrian Orthodox Church is very old. It follows the liturgy of St James the Less which is still read in the ancient language of Syriac. After the schism of Chalcedon the Syrian Orthodox became known as Jacobites after Jacob Baradai who expanded the Monophysite doctrine. For many of the early pilgrims from Europe, Jacobite was the name for all Eastern Orthodox Christians. The Syrian community became

Father.
Yacoub.

Yacoub means to
follow.

very wealthy to the extent that it is said they bought the Church of the Holy Sepulchre from the Saracens for a large sum of gold. In 1587 their good fortune ended. Bishop Youhana forbade his sexton to marry a close relative. The sexton, mad with anguish and revenge, took the bishop's shoe and printed the name 'Mohammed' on the bottom. He then went to the Turkish authorities and told them that the Syrian bishop would only celebrate Mass if he trod on the name 'Mohammed'. The officials found the shoe with the name on it and the bishop was hung in front of the Syrian Monastery of the Lentils. The Moslems then took their revenge on the Syrians. Many were killed, a number hastily converted to Islam or joined other Orthodox

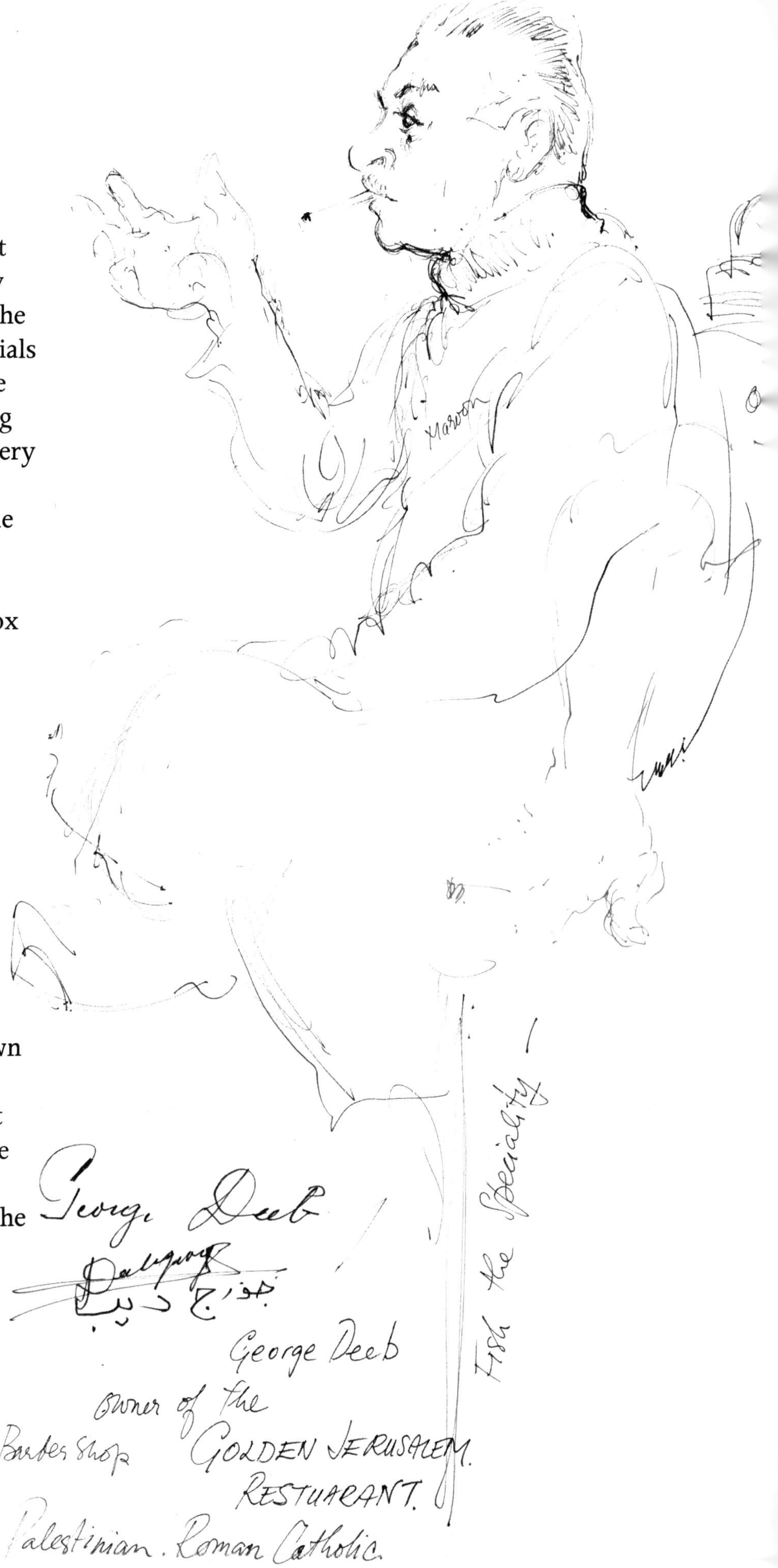

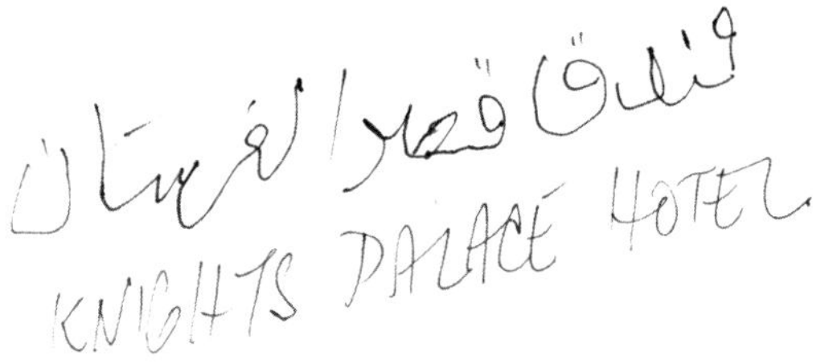

Churches, the rest were thrown out of Jerusalem. The community is now quite small. At St Mark's Monastery there are only three monks, a bishop and twenty or so deacons at the seminary.

فندق قصر الفرسان
KNIGHTS PALACE HOTEL

Maroon

George Deeb

George Deeb
owner of the
GOLDEN JERUSALEM.
RESTUARANT.
Palestinian. Roman Catholic.

in the Barber shop

Fish the Speciality

The Silver Smith of.
The "SILVER STAR".

Nimer

Mr Nimer = Tiger.
Syrian formerly from
Turkey.

SILVER SMITH
NIMER N. HERRO

Father Yacoub was born in
Mesopotamia and has been in
Jerusalem for twelve years. He
is a large, dark man who speaks
excellent English having studied
at an Anglican seminary outside
Leeds. The monastery is rela-
tively new but it stands on the
site of St Mark's House. It was
here that St Peter knocked on
the door after he was released
from prison. On the wall of the
room where we sit is an inscription in Syriac. Father
Yacoub translates for me:

> 'In the house of St Mark all
> old things were completed.
> That night the old way of
> killing animals was stopped.
> There a new covenant was
> established. And in this way
> old heresies were refuted.'

According to the Syrians,
the Last Supper was eaten here
and the old rules about animal
sacrifices were replaced. The
rest of the Orthodox Churches
say that the Last Supper was
eaten on Mount Zion so that
this has been a matter of con-
tention between them and the
Syrians.

Father Yacoub seems intent
to impress me with the historical
rights of the Syrians in the Old

City. Father Ilias is summoned to write the prayer in Syriac under my drawing. He is darker and more hawk-like than Father Yacoub and is the scribe for the monastery. While he writes, Father Yacoub explains about the cap the Syrians wear which is joined at the back to the cassock. It is the symbol of the monastic order of St Antonios and can only be worn by celibates. Father Ilias finishes. Without ruled lines he has copied exactly the inscription in the intricate Syriac script, an amazing bit of penmanship.

There are Protestants in the Old City too. The Anglicans and Lutherans have churches but no rights to the Holy Sepulchre, though the Greek Orthodox do permit the Anglicans to hold one service a year in one of their chapels. The Anglican Archbishop is termed Archbishop 'in' Jerusalem, not 'of' so as not to offend the Christian Orthodox.

I have also seen black Baptists from the United States in the Old City—they hold sing-songs in the Garden of Gethsemane—as well as a contingent of shaven-headed Buddhist monks in saffron robes.

SALMAN

EXCLUSIVE JEWELLERY or SOUVENIR

OLD CITY BAZAAR

NATIVE BAZAAR

HOLY SEP

Dabbagha.
(Dye)
old Turkish.

(Suq AFTIMOS
(Aftimos Market)
Belongs to Greek Orthodox

Suq Ed Dabbagha St & Muristan on left, outside Holy Sepulchre.

Omri Ben-Avraham עמרי בן אברהם
קיבוץ עין-שמר

In the Parachute Division.
Done one year. — another 2 years to go
from Kibutz Ein-Shemer

The word Jerusalem means Peace, but peace is what has
eluded the city since its beginnings.
The sound of a bomb going off in a distant street, a group of
soldiers standing guard at the gates, Arabs being searched,
riot squads and more soldiers on rooftops, are all too much of a reminder
that still this city does not live up to its name.

Before the Israeli soldier there was a Jordanian doing the same duties,
before him an Englishman, a Turk, a Crusader, a Saracen, a Roman, a
Persian, for Jerusalem provokes and has provoked too many passions and
too much violence.

What problems it has had to encounter! For one city to be the focal
point of Judaism, of Christianity and of Islam, compounded by political
and territorial arguments, must make it one of the most bitterly disputed
cities in the world.

Take Christianity: it seemed simple in the beginning, one religion
united against a common enemy, but then came official recognition from
Emperor Constantine who received divine revelation whilst marching
through Italy in the year 312.

Soon the Eastern Orthodox Church split, Greek Orthodox from the
rest; they in turn separated from the Roman Catholics, and all over
matters of doctrine and dogma. They are still arguing today. The official

branding by Emperor Theodosius II of the Jews as anti-Christ, the fanaticism of the Crusaders towards Jew and Moslem alike; to this day no Orthodox Jew will pass in front of the Holy Sepulchre; and the arguments and controversies between the Churches themselves, Coptic against Ethiopian, Syrian against Armenian.

corner of Al wad & Khan Ez-zeit just inside
Damascus gate.

The Jews arguing amongst
themselves, one yeshiva dis-
puting the teaching of the other,
the intolerance of the religious
towards the secular, the refusal
of one group of Orthodox to
accept even the State of Israel.
No group seems exempt from its
form of prejudice.

The Moslems persecuted
both Christians and Jews during

shared amenities of water, bath-
room and kitchen. One family
I visited sent one of their sons to
the Frères Roman Catholic
school, the other to the Lutheran

The Christian secular population live together peacefully even if their Churches are split. Many of the Christian Arabs live in compounds, a cluster of rooms around a courtyard with

Turkish times; more recently,
during the British Mandate,
there were incidents of religious
fanatics killing Jews praying at
the Wailing Wall which resulted
in Jewish retaliation and then
open warfare; five wars since
1948 between the two peoples.
Jews were forbidden access to
their shrines under the Jordanians, while Arab houses were
razed by Israelis after the
Six Day War. Even so, there
are other signs.

Herb – Vegetable Sellers

and their daughter to the Greek Orthodox. The father is a Roman Catholic, while the mother was baptized into the Greek Orthodox Church but like many Arab women has converted to her husband's faith. Their neighbours are Greek Catholics, Coptic and Syrian Orthodox. They live in the middle of the Moslem Quarter.

Under Israeli law there is complete freedom for everyone to follow his chosen creed without persecution from others.

Pilgrims come from all countries, Arab as well, to pay homage at their shrines; no one is banned.

In the souks the shopkeepers, Christian and Moslem, work side by side and the different ethnic groups respect each other. When sketching them there is much conversation and the inevitable question, 'What are you?'

'I'm Arab.'

'I'm Jewish.'

'I'm Syrian.'

'I'm Palestinian.'

'I'm Greek.'

'I'm Israeli.'

'I'm Armenian.'

Bab-el-Silseleh
Gate.

Main Gate.

But I never once heard, 'I'm a Jerusalemite.'

At other times I was swamped by children. Those romping screeching large-eyed bundles of humanity who play and cavort around the corners and walls of the Old City. They surrounded me, obstructed my view, jabbed dirty fingers at my lines, passed me my inks, ran for cigarettes.

And when one piped up and
asked me, 'What are you?'
there was an immediate response
from his fellows: 'He's an artist,
silly.'
    They are the future of
Jerusalem.

Chronological Table

BC

1000	'The City Of David', capital of the Kingdom of Israel
931	The disruption of Solomon's kingdom which becomes the Kingdom of Judah and Israel
722	End of the Kingdom of Israel and start of the Assyrian Empire
597	Babylonians capture Jerusalem and first diaspora starts
539	Cyrus the Great captures Jerusalem. The Jews begin to return
520–516	The Temple is rebuilt
333	Alexander the Great captures Palestine and the Hellenistic period starts
312	Ptolemy Egyptian Dynasty starts
198	The beginning of the Greek domination of Palestine as the Seleucids take over Jerusalem
141	Jerusalem captured by Hasmoneans
63	The Romans under Pompey settle the Near East
37–4	Herod the Great's reign under Pompey

AD

c.29	Jesus Christ crucified
66–70	First great Jewish revolt
135	Jerusalem rebuilt by Romans as Aelia Capitolina
312	Emperor Constantine arrives in Jerusalem
325–335	Church of Holy Sepulchre built
614	Persian Sassanians overrun Jerusalem
630	The Emperor Heraclius restores Jerusalem to Byzantine rule

632	Death of Mohammed
634	Caliph Omar arrives in Jerusalem
688	Dome of the Rock built during the Caliphate of Abd-ul-Malik
1099	Crusaders capture Jerusalem during the First Crusade
1187	Salāh ad-Dīn takes Jerusalem from Crusaders
1260	The defeat of the Tartars by Mamlūke Sultan Qutuz and Frankish allies
1517	Mamelūkes defeated by the Turks
1517–1918	Turkish rule in Jerusalem